When Jennife[...] t the angels of abundant [...] excitement. The Lord has been speaking to me about the upgrades that He has for His people. In this book you will not only hear the word for this season, but also you will receive much needed insight into the angelic realm. Angels are assigned to bring forth blessing and breakthrough. One angel encounter can shift your life! Get ready to be elevated, empowered, and aligned.

—RYAN LESTRANGE
FOUNDER, IMPACT INTERNATIONAL
PRESIDENT, NEW BREED REVIVAL NETWORK
COFOUNDER, AWAKENINGTV.COM

Jennifer LeClaire has brought forth a now word concerning angels through a biblical foundation and clear understanding of the purpose of angels for the creative service to God and in the aiding and assisting of mankind. As you read this book, you will discover the greater role that angels have in the kingdom and your personal, day-to-day life. Although our generation has seen an increase of spiritual warfare and demonic spirits so that it has become the norm in our culture, this book will equip you in advancing the kingdom of God as a son or daughter of God. As you read, you will be reminded, encouraged, and equipped to know that angels have been assigned, purposed, and destined for you. You will no longer see angels as figurines on a fireplace mantle but as an advantage for kingdom increase. An abundance of angelic presence is about to be released into your identity!

—Ryan Johnson
Founder, Ryan Johnson Ministries

In *Releasing the Angels of Abundant Harvest* Jennifer offers a prophetic plumb line that rightly divides the Word for believers on how to discern and deploy angelic assistance to reap a harvest for kingdom advancement.

—Jason Armstrong
President, Remnant Fire Ministries

Many believers in this hour do not understand the importance of angelic assistance in their everyday walk and assignments. There is a great need for this revelation in the body of Christ, and I believe this book explains how and why angelic assistance is needed today.

—Ricky Scaparo
Founder, EndtimeHeadlines.org

A
PROPHETIC
WORD
for
RADICAL
INCREASE
in 2017

RELEASING
the
ANGELS
of
ABUNDANT
HARVEST

JENNIFER LeCLAIRE

CHARISMA
HOUSE

Most Charisma House Book Group products are available at special quantity discounts for bulk purchase for sales promotions, premiums, fund-raising, and educational needs. For details, write Charisma House Book Group, 600 Rinehart Road, Lake Mary, Florida 32746, or telephone (407) 333-0600.

Releasing the Angels of Abundant Harvest
  by Jennifer LeClaire
Published by Charisma House
Charisma Media/Charisma House Book Group
600 Rinehart Road
Lake Mary, Florida 32746
www.charismahouse.com

Cover design by Lisa Rae McClure
Design Director: Justin Evans

Visit the author's website at www.jenniferleclaire.org.

Library of Congress Control Number: 2016960916
International Standard Book Number: 978-1-62999-176-4
E-book ISBN: 978-1-62999-177-1

While the author has made every effort to provide accurate Internet addresses at the time of publication, neither the publisher nor the author assumes any responsibility for errors or for changes that occur after publication.

17 18 19 20 21 — 987654321
Printed in the United States of America

CONTENTS

FOREWORD

My ears perk up every time I hear that Jennifer LeClaire is releasing another book. Why? Her writings are grounded scripturally, abound in research, and contain the third needed strand of contemporary experience. Guess what? That is how exactly I write! So finding a next generation voice that combines these same three strands that I have attempted to uphold in the global prayer and prophetic movements brings great joy to my heart!

In 1993 the angelic armies invaded my home in suburban Missouri for nine straight weeks from midnight to 5:00 a.m. Yes, every night. I had read and studied all three hundred verses in the Bible on angels three different times over three different decades. Then a prophetic explosion of the manifested presence of God took place in our home and impacted my family in every imaginable way. Eventually the book *Angelic Encounters* was birthed, telling some of these encounters. I trust that the book has been used to help ground people as I referenced over two hundred Bibles verses while fanning the flame of "More, Lord" for today.

It is another day, another hour. It is harvest time! I now feel we have an appropriate sequel to *Angelic Encounters* in the book *Releasing the Angels of Abundant Harvest* by my trusted friend Jennifer LeClaire. I exposed the reader to encounters of a heavenly kind and now Jennifer exposes you to partnering with the heavenly hosts for the purpose of the harvest! Yes, the missing link has now been appropriated! Praise the Lord!

I concur with the exhortation in the opening chapter and the prophetic word "I am releasing the angels of abundant harvest." Yes and amen! As I stated previously, it is harvest time. Not only does this book inspire you, but it also engages you with tools of activation. In fact, there are additional noteworthy chapters such as "Activating Angelic Ministry in Your Life" and "Prophetic Declarations That Release Angels." These writings bring you tools within boundaries!

Then one of the primary reasons I am thrilled to highly recommend this book to you is that Jennifer has so wisely included the material found in the chapter "Avoiding Angelic Deceptions." This complements material I have taught for years around the globe about nine scriptural tests that I believe all prophetic encounters should be subjected to. Thank you, Jennifer!

So you see, right now at this vantage point in life, as a father in the prayer and prophetic movement, I now get to help coach others and occasionally even be a cheerleader when I find someone I really want to give a shout to. It is a great honor and privilege to commend to you this tool, this amazing manual, this inspirational book titled *Releasing the Angels of Abundant Harvest.* This book contains the rest of what I want to say!

Blessings to each of you!

—Dr. James W. Goll
God Encounters Ministries
International Speaker and Author

Chapter 1

I AM RELEASING THE ANGELS OF ABUNDANT HARVEST

Hear the word of the Lord:

An abundant harvest is at hand. I am releasing angels of abundant harvest into the nation. You will reap what you have sown. This is a double-edged sword.

Where the enemy has resisted your harvest in years past, you will see a multiplication effect of blessing in your life. Doors will open unto you that no man can open. Opportunities will come your way that you never dreamed, imagined, or even thought to ask for. Provision will enter your life from unexpected places.

If you have sown to the Spirit, you will reap from the Spirit. If you have sown into My kingdom business, you will see a return on the investment of your time, your finances, and your relationships. Reinforcement will come to support the work of your hand. You will find that lack is no longer in your language. You will see blessings chase you down and overtake you.

You will find that I am leading you and guiding you with greater precision. You will hear My voice and dream My dreams and see My visions. You will rest in Me and have confidence and faith in Me that defies the enemy's plans for your life. This is a year of abundant harvest.

I will not be mocked. Whatever a man sows, he will reap. There are laws of the harvest, and they are in effect.

If you have been holding back what belongs to Me, release it. If you have been muzzling the ox, loose him. If you have been sowing seeds of discord among My children, go to them in humility and make it right. If you have been defying My will, get in alignment with Me now.

I am releasing the angels of abundant harvest. They will minister blessings to the heirs of salvation. They will bring provision and protection from the enemy's sword. I am releasing the angels of abundant harvest. Make your choice. Choose this day whom you will serve with your whole heart. I am a God of justice. I am also a God of mercy.

You have put Me to the test in the last season, and a season of abundant harvest is coming into your life. Prepare your hearts now to receive what is in store for you. I am your God, and I love you with an everlasting love. I am releasing angels of abundant harvest.

WHY I'M RELEASING THIS
WORD WITH GODLY FEAR

When I received this prophetic word from the Lord, I immediately began to measure it against the plumb line of the written Word of God—the Scripture. The fear of the Lord constrains me from hopping on extreme teachings on angels with New Age names and operations that are so far beyond the bounds of the Bible that they lead people into error, even if the experience was valid.

I believe some spiritual encounters need to be kept private if they do not edify the body of Christ—and especially if they suggest new doctrines, cause people to chase after supernatural realms instead of the God of the supernatural realm, or breed strong confusion among believers. Although I agree that some legitimate supernatural experiences are not necessarily mirrored in Scripture and I certainly do not want to put God in a religious box, there is wisdom on what we share publicly and what we keep private.

We also need to be good Bereans and examine the Scriptures to see if our experience agrees with the spirit of the Word (Acts 17:11). After all, the Holy Spirit and the Word agree (1 John 5:8).

I could go on and on about the serious words in Jeremiah 23, but let me leave you with this one that acts as a sobering introduction to Paul's exhortation in Colossians: "I have heard what the prophets say who prophesy lies in my name. They say, 'I had a dream! I had a dream!' How long will this continue in the hearts of these lying prophets, who prophesy the delusions of their own minds? They think the dreams they tell one another will make my people forget my name, just as their ancestors forgot my name through Baal worship" (Jer. 23:25–27, NIV).

In Colossians 2:18–19 Paul clearly warned: "Do not let anyone who delights in false humility and the worship of angels disqualify you. Such a person also goes into great detail about what they have seen; they are puffed up with idle notions by their unspiritual mind. They have lost connection with the head, from whom the whole body, supported and held together by its ligaments and sinews, grows as God causes it to grow" (NIV).

These sorts of scriptures put the fear of the Lord in me. I do not want to be among the lying prophets. I do not want to prophesy delusions of my own mind. I do not want to be puffed up with notions of my unspiritual mind. I do not want to lose connection with the head. So I weigh and judge and examine and scrutinize prophecies before I release them—and invite other more experienced leaders to do the same. And they have done so with this prophetic word.

That said, once the spirit is tested and the word deemed accurate, I do not want to hold it back. I want to release it in the Lord's perfect timing. After all, Jeremiah 23:28–29 says, "'Let the prophet who has a dream recount the dream, but let the one who has my word speak it faithfully. For what has straw to do with grain?' declares the LORD. 'Is not my word like fire,' declares the LORD, 'and like a hammer that breaks a rock in pieces?'" (NIV).

We should not prophesy vanity, but holding back a prophetic word that could cause people to miss a visitation or encounter judgment is irresponsible.

BIBLICAL PRINCIPLES IN THE ABUNDANT ANGEL PROPHECY

With that, let's measure this prophecy against the plumb line of Scripture before we move on to its application in the chapters ahead. The concept of abundant harvest is repeated in God's Word. Proverbs 14:4 tells us, "Where there are no oxen, the manger is empty, but from the strength of an ox come abundant harvests" (NIV). *Harvests* there is plural, clearly suggesting an abundant harvest is not a one-time event. You can have many abundant harvests in your life, just as you can have many lean years.

In Luke 12:16–21, Jesus told a parable about a rich man who yielded an abundant harvest. The idea in this parable was that the rich man kept building bigger and bigger barns to store his wealth but was not rich toward God. Jesus frowned on this behavior. Luke 10:2 (HCSB) speaks of an abundant harvest in the context of souls ready to hear the Word, and Jesus bemoans that the laborers are few and issues a prayer charge to send workers into the harvest.

But there is a flip side to the abundant harvest as the prophecy indicates. Nehemiah 9:36–37 says, "But see, we are slaves today, slaves in the land you gave our ancestors so they could eat its fruit and the other good things it produces. Because of our sins, its abundant harvest goes to the kings you have placed over us. They rule over our bodies and our cattle as they please. We are in great distress" (NIV).

In other words, God's people who were practicing sin reaped the reward of that sin and their abundant harvest went to the enemy. God had set up the Israelites for abundant harvest—plentiful provision—but because they refused to serve Him and looked to idols and neglected numerous opportunities to repent, they walked into bondage and the enemy claimed their increase. Thank God, we can go boldly to the throne of grace and find mercy and grace to help in our time of need (Heb. 4:16). If you have been withholding your time and resources from the Lord, now is the time to repent and set things right with Him. God desires mercy over judgment (James 2:13).

The prophetic word suggested those who have been sowing to the Spirit yet have been met with enemy resistance will see a multiplication effect of blessing in their lives. This is scriptural. When you sow into good ground, you will produce a harvest—some thirty-, sixty-, or even a hundredfold (Matt. 13:8). When Isaac sowed in the land where the Lord directed him, he reaped in that same year a hundredfold with the Lord's blessing (Gen. 26:12).

I believe the reinforcement of which the prophecy speaks is people and angels. Psalm 103:20 tells us God's mighty angels hearken to the voice of His Word. Put another way, they execute God's Word. The New Living Translation says they "[listen] for each of His commands." The Message Bible reveals His angels are "ready and able to fly at his bidding, quick to hear and do what he says." God has angel armies ready to respond to His will in a moment. Those who have sown to the Spirit—who have been obedient despite trials and tribulations and naysayers—will see blessing chase them down and overtake them, according to the promise in Deuteronomy 28:2.

The prophecy says God will lead and guide the one who has sown to the Spirit with greater precision and prophetic experiences. When we cultivate intimacy with Him—when we lean back on Jesus's breast and pursue friendship with Him—we will hear Him more clearly. Jesus said, "I no longer call you servants, for a servant does not know what his master does. But I have called you friends, for everything that I have heard from My Father have I made known to you" (John 15:15). In this hour of history there will be a marked difference between those who walk as servants only and those who also walk as friends of God.

God is releasing angels of abundant harvest. Angels are ministering spirits sent to serve those who are the heirs of salvation (Heb. 1:14). Angels can bring provision, according to Scripture. We'll explore that more in the next chapter.

Many believers stand in the Valley of Shechem. Listen closely to the heart of the prophetic message Joshua delivered to Israel on that day of decision—then apply it to yourself:

> Now therefore, fear the LORD, serve Him in sincerity and in truth, and put away the gods which your fathers served on the other side of the River and in Egypt. Serve the LORD! And if it seems evil to you to serve the LORD, choose for yourselves this day whom you will serve, whether the gods which your fathers served that were on the other side of the River, or the gods of the Amorites, in whose land you dwell. But as for me and my house, we will serve the LORD.
>
> —JOSHUA 24:14–15, NKJV

Now is a *kairos* time. It's a season of the release of angels of abundant harvest. Those who are serving the Lord with right motives are about to see an abundant harvest, according to the measure they've sown in obedience. God is releasing the angels to bring in the harvest.

Chapter 2

WHAT ANGELS ACTUALLY DO

Before 2016 even began, the Holy Spirit expressly told me it would be a year of shifting seasons and suddenlies. That means transitions. Throughout 2016 many reported shifting seasons, suddenlies, and transitions—or felt one coming on. Others experienced strong frustration because they bore witness to the prophetic word but felt stuck in a vicious circle or demonic cycle that manifested in warfare and delays. Later in 2016 the Holy Spirit shed some light on how angels can minister to us in times of transition. Consider what He told me:

> Many neglect the angels of transition, and they bypass the help I have sent to transition them into the next stage of their journey. Many ignore the angels of transition and therefore fail to enter into the new place I have set aside for them at the appointed time. Many are working in their own strength, struggling in the flesh, and failing to embrace the work of My angels on assignment to help them transition into the new thing. Look for the angels in times of transition.

Only God can transition you from glory to glory, but there are angels to help you. Despite the acknowledged extreme teachings in the realm of angels, I was surprised at how much angelic activity we find in both the Old and New Testaments. Angels are mentioned 108 times in the Old Testament and 165 times in the New Testament—and the New Testament is much shorter!

I believe we are neglecting this powerful resource. We certainly do not worship angels, but it's absolutely foolish to ignore their ministry. Let me show you some ways angels can help in times of transition.

You Have an Angel

In Matthew 18:10 Jesus said, "See that you do not despise one of these little ones. For I say to you that in heaven their angels always see the face of My Father who is in heaven."

Angelic activity was common in the New Testament. After an angel released Peter from prison, Peter came knocking on the door where intercessors were fervently praying for his release—but these prayer warriors didn't believe when the man of God actually showed up! They said, "It is his angel" (Acts 12:15). The Bible says angels are ministering spirits to those who inherit salvation (Heb. 1:14).

We focus so much on demons, but remember, only one-third of the angels fell. Two-thirds are still on our side. We need to understand the ministry of angels.

Angels can offer information.

Angel really means "messenger," so this is one of the primary functions of an angel:

- Gabriel announced the birth of John the Baptist (Luke 1:5–25).

- Gabriel announced the birth of Jesus (Luke 1:26–38).

- God used angels to interpret visions He gave to Daniel, Zechariah, and John in the Book of Revelation.

- Angels shared with the shepherds the location of Christ's birthplace in the manger (Luke 2:8–20).

- An angel warned Joseph to flee to Egypt because Herod wanted to kill the child Jesus (Matt. 2:13).

- An angel announced Christ's resurrection to the women who found His empty tomb (John 20).

Angels can offer direction.

An angel directed Abraham's servant in Genesis 24:1–7 to find a wife for Abraham's son. Abraham told him, "He shall send His angel before you and you shall take a wife for my son from there" (v. 7). The angel directed the servant straight to Rebekah.

An angel directed Philip in Acts 8:26: "Now an angel of the Lord said to Philip, 'Rise up and go toward the south on the way that goes down from Jerusalem to Gaza.'"

An angel directed Cornelius to call for Peter in Acts 10:3–5: "About the ninth hour of the day he saw clearly in a vision an angel of God coming in and saying to him, 'Cornelius.' When he looked at him he was afraid, and said, 'What is it, Lord?' He said to him, 'Your prayers and your alms have come up as a memorial before God. Now send men to Joppa, and bring back Simon whose surname is Peter.'"

Angels can protect you.

An angel protected Daniel in the lion's den in Daniel 6:19–22. Daniel told the king, "My God has sent His angel and has shut the lions' mouths so that they have not hurt me, because innocence was found in me before Him; and also before you, O king, I have done no harm" (v. 22).

An angel protected Shadrach, Meshach, and Abednego in the fiery furnace in Daniel 3:26–29. The Bible says God "sent His angel and delivered His servants who trusted in Him. They have defied the king's word, and yielded their bodies, that they might not serve nor worship any god, except their own God" (v. 28).

The Lord spoke to Moses sternly about angelic protection in Exodus 23:20–22: "Indeed, I am going to send an angel before you to guard you along the way and to bring you into the place which I have prepared. Be on guard before him and obey his voice. Do not provoke him, for he will not pardon your transgressions, for My name is in him. But if you diligently obey his voice and do all that I say, then I will be an enemy to your enemies and an adversary to your adversaries."

Angels can bring provision.

An angel provided water for Hagar after Abraham expelled her in Genesis 21:15–19. An angel brought Elijah food after his battle with the false prophets and his run from Jezebel in 1 Kings 19:5–6: "As he lay and slept under the juniper tree, an angel touched him and said to him, 'Arise and eat.' He looked, and there was a cake baked on coals and a jar of water at his head. And he ate and drank and then lay down again."

Angels can war on your behalf.

God sent an angel to fight for Israel in 2 Kings 19:35: "On that night the angel of the LORD went out and struck one hundred and eighty-five thousand in the camp of the Assyrians. When others woke up early in the morning, these were all dead bodies." And God showed Elisha's servant the angel armies that stood with them in 2 Kings 6:15–17.

Angels can also bring in a harvest (Matt. 13:39), bring judgment (1 Chron. 21:15), assist in healing (John 5:3–4), and bring encouragement (Dan. 9:21). Angels are worshippers. This is not an exhaustive study of angels, but you can see how active they are in the spirit realm and some of the biblical operations. There are angels of abundant harvest!

Chapter 3

WHAT ARE YOU SOWING?

New Agers call it karma. Psychics call it fortune or fate. Indeed, there are many ways people describe what is ultimately a spiritual law that works the same for all creation. So let me ask you an important question: What are you sowing?

Paul the apostle perhaps describes God's divine statute most succinctly in Galatians 6:7–9: "Be not deceived. God is not mocked. For whatever a man sows, that will he also reap. For the one who sows to his own flesh will from the flesh reap corruption, but the one who sows to the Spirit will from the Spirit reap eternal life. And let us not grow weary in doing good, for in due season we shall reap, if we do not give up."

I appreciate the Amplified Bible, Classic Edition's translation of this verse: "Do not be deceived and deluded and misled; God will not allow Himself to be sneered at (scorned, disdained, or mocked by mere pretensions or professions, or by His precepts being set aside.) [He inevitably deludes himself who attempts to delude God.] For whatever a man sows, that and that only is what he will reap. For he who sows to his own flesh (lower nature, sensuality) will from the flesh reap decay and ruin and destruction, but he who sows to the Spirit will from the Spirit reap eternal life. And let us not lose heart and grow weary and faint in acting nobly and doing right, for in due time and at the appointed season we shall reap, if we do not loosen and relax our courage and faint."

What a clear warning! Here's one more version—a translation from *The Message* Bible—just to drive the point home: "Don't be misled: No one makes a fool of God. What a person plants, he will harvest. The person who plants selfishness, ignoring the needs of others— ignoring God!—harvests a crop of weeds. All he'll have to show for his life is weeds! But the one who plants in response to God, letting God's Spirit do the growth work in him, harvests a crop of real life, eternal life. So let's not allow ourselves to get fatigued doing good. At the right time we will harvest a good crop if we don't give up, or quit. Right now, therefore, every time we get the chance, let us work for the benefit of all, starting with the people closest to us in the community of faith."

WHAT ARE YOU SOWING?

God is releasing the angels of abundant harvest. That's good news—if you've been sowing. Stop for a moment and consider your ways in this season. The Lord wants to deliver abundance into your storehouse, but you need to give Him something to work with. At a *kairos* time such as this we don't want to be like the Israelites in Haggai's day:

> Now, therefore, thus says the LORD of Hosts: Consider your ways. You have sown much, and harvested little. You eat, but you do not have enough; you drink, but you are not filled with drink; you clothe yourselves, but no one is warm; and he who earns wages earns wages to put them into a bag with holes.
>
> Thus says the LORD of Hosts: Consider your ways. Go up to the mountain and bring wood and rebuild the house, that I may take pleasure in it and be glorified, says the LORD. You looked for much, and it came to little; and when you brought it home, I blew it away. Why? says the LORD of Hosts. Because of My house that lies in ruins while each of you runs to his own house. Therefore the heavens above you have withheld the dew, and the earth has withheld its crops. I called for a drought on the land and the mountains, on the grain, on the new wine, on the oil, on what the ground brings forth, on men, on livestock, and on all the labor of your hands.
>
> —HAGGAI 1:5–11

We need to consider our ways. We need to be about God's kingdom business in this hour. Now more than ever, we need to seek first His kingdom and His righteousness and believe everything we need will be added to us (Matt. 6:33). That means sowing our time and financial resources in the ground to which God leads us.

In spiritual warfare circles we like to declare "the kingdom of God suffers violence and the violent must take it by force." (See Matthew 11:12.) But did you know one translation of the Greek word *force* in that scripture means to "claim for one's self eagerly," according to the *KJV New Testament Greek Lexicon?*[1] It's time to sow eagerly and know that in doing so, we position ourselves to claim eagerly the abundant harvest that God has stored up for us in every area of our lives.

Many have been declaring Proverbs 13:22 for decades: "The wealth of the sinner is laid up for the just." I believe we're entering into a Proverbs 13:22 season where a wealth transfer will begin to happen before our eyes. But that wealth transfer does not supersede the truth in Galatians 6:7–9. You will reap what you sow. So if you haven't been sowing, you are not aligned for a supernatural wealth transfer. The good news is that it's not too late to sow. What's more, the law of harvest is not restricted to wealth. The Bible says that whatever a man sows, he will reap.

STOP ROBBING ME!

You may have heard my testimony. In brief, my husband abandoned me and our two-year-old baby. Shortly after that I was falsely accused of a crime I did not commit and landed in jail for forty days while they were sorting it out. I was eventually vindicated and the slate was wiped clean, but when I emerged from jail, I had next to nothing.

I spent almost every penny I had paying an attorney who would actually fight for me after the first attorney bailed with my money. The dot-com bubble burst, so I lost my livelihood. My parents thought I was going up the river for five years, so they got rid of my apartment and my dog. I came out of the jail with nothing except my newfound faith in Christ.

My wilderness journey led me to Alabama, where I wound up on food stamps because I was impoverished. Still, I had a generous heart. I saw people who were worse off than I was—there's always someone worse off than you—and when they would ask me to borrow money, I obliged out of the goodness of my heart. Not one of them paid me back! I was frustrated and upset because I really didn't have the money to lose.

I still remember the day I got down on my knees, kneeling over my bright red couch and complaining to God. I was whining and groaning and moaning about how everyone was robbing me. I was explaining that I was helping people with pure motives and was being robbed. I made it very clear that I was sick and tired of people robbing me. Suddenly that still small voice whispered five words to my spirit: "Then stop robbing from Me."

That startled me. I didn't know what He meant. I was just newly born again, a babe in Christ. I had never heard of tithing. I knew nothing about sowing and reaping. I didn't understand the concept of love offerings or sacrificial giving. But you'd better believe I was a quick study. I got in the Word and found the answers I needed to begin sowing my way out of poverty. Today I am debt free and own several properties. Although I worked hard, I believe I sowed my way to prosperity through giving of my finances and my time—putting the kingdom first.

PUTTING THE LORD TO THE TEST

If you haven't been sowing your time and resources into the kingdom, it's time to consider your ways and return to the Lord. Malachi 3:7–16 gives us God's perspective on this:

> Return to Me, and I will return to you, says the LORD of Hosts. But you say, "How shall we return?" Will a man rob God? Yet you have robbed Me. But you say, "How have we robbed You?" In tithes and offerings. You are cursed with a curse, your whole nation, for you are robbing Me.
>
> Bring all the tithes into the storehouse, that there may be food in My house, and test Me now in this, says the LORD of Hosts, if I will not open for you the windows of heaven and pour out for you a blessing, that there will not be room enough to receive it. I will rebuke the devourer for your sakes, so that it will not

destroy the fruit of your ground, and the vines in your field will not fail to bear fruit, says the Lord of Hosts. Then all the nations will call you blessed, for you will be a delightful land, says the Lord of Hosts.

Your words have been hard against Me, says the Lord. Yet you say, "What have we spoken against You?"

You said, "It is vain to serve God. What profit is it that we have kept His ordinance, and that we have walked as mourners before the Lord of Hosts? And now we call the proud blessed, for those who do wickedness are built up; they even test God and escape." Then those who feared the Lord spoke to one another. The Lord listened and heard them, and a book of remembrance was written before Him for those who fear the Lord and who esteem His name.

Nowhere else in Scripture do we see an invitation to test the Lord. Test the Lord now. Begin to sow now. God will surely open the windows of heaven and pour out for you a blessing—spiritual and natural—bigger than anything you could ever imagine if you obey Him. What's more, He will also rebuke the devourer that was plaguing the Israelites in Haggai's day. He wants to show you there is profit in serving Him. Don't hold back your gifts and talents—sow them into the kingdom. Don't hold back your offerings—sow what He puts on your heart. Do everything as unto the Lord. He will do His part if you do your part.

So again, what are you sowing?

Chapter 4

DEMYSTIFYING THE LAW OF ABUNDANCE

I GREW UP WITH plenty—more than enough, actually. My family was not wealthy, but there was always an abundance. When I moved out at age eighteen, defying my parents' wishes to attend university in Dallas, I experienced true lack for the first time in my life. I whittled down to about ninety-five pounds—and I'm five foot seven—before I finally decided to go live with my grandparents.

When I married my college sweetheart, we prospered financially. For twentysomethings, we were abounding, making what some today would call "mad money." He was a photographer, and I was a journalist. We had nice cars, cell phones before most people had cell phones, and just about whatever else we wanted. When he abandoned me and our then-two-year-old baby, it was the beginning of another season of lack.

You've heard part of my testimony. I lost almost every penny I had trying to secure my freedom from the false accusations and wound up in the wilderness on food stamps. Needless to say, this was not the abundant life Christ died to give me. But I worked hard, I was careful to be a giver, and God rebuilt my life—every area of my life—on His terms. Within a few years of this abasement I was again abounding. I had learned to activate the law of abundance.

Today I own two condos I paid cash for and am 100 percent debt free. I'm not a millionaire, but I am abounding in prosperity—and it's not just finances. I've embraced the reality of John 10:10, "The thief does not come, except to steal and kill and destroy. I came that they may have life, and that they may have it more abundantly." I am more than a little familiar with the thief's stealing, killing, and destroying agenda. But I'm also more than a little familiar with the reality of Christ's promise of an abundant life. I like the latter better.

As a matter of fact, the Amplified translation of John 10:10 paints a clearer picture of what Jesus was saying to His disciples: "I came that they may have and enjoy life, and have it in abundance (to the full, till it overflows)" (AMPC). Jesus came to give us an enjoyable life, an abundant life, a full life—an overflowing life. Although it's possible to have an enjoyable life without abundance, when you activate the law of abundance in your life as I did in mine, you'll discover a deeper revelation of Luke 6:38.

In fact, Luke 6:38 is essentially another spin on Galatians 6:7's "reap what you sow" law: "Give, and it will be given to you: Good measure, pressed down, shaken together, and running over will men give unto you. For with the measure you use, it will be measured unto you."

Again, this is not just in the matter of finances. Jesus wants you to be in health and prosper even as your soul prospers (3 John 1:2). When your soul prospers, you will find the abundant life Christ died to deliver you into—an enjoyable life, a full life, an overflowing life where you walk in the promises of God.

Living in the Overflow

God wants health to overflow in your life. He wants strong friendships, marriage, and family to be enjoyable. He wants your vocation to be prosperous, whether in the ministry or in the marketplace. Deuteronomy 28:3–14 describes the life God wants to see you live when you walk in obedience to His Word, which activates the law of abundance:

> You will be blessed in the city and blessed in the field. Your offspring will be blessed, and the produce of your ground, and the offspring of your livestock, the increase of your herd and the flocks of your sheep. Your basket and your kneading bowl will be blessed. You will be blessed when you come in and blessed when you go out.
>
> The Lord will cause your enemies who rise up against you to be defeated before you; they will come out against you one way and flee before you seven ways. The Lord will command the blessing on you in your barns and in all that you

set your hand to do, and He will bless you in the land which the LORD your God is giving you.

The LORD will establish you as a holy people to Himself, just as He swore to you, if you will keep the commandments of the LORD your God and walk in His ways. All people of the earth shall see that you are called by the name of the LORD, and they shall be afraid of you. The LORD will make you overflow in prosperity, in the offspring of your body, in the offspring of your livestock, and in the produce of your ground, in the land which the LORD swore to your fathers to give you.

The LORD will open up to you His good treasure, the heavens, to give the rain to your land in its season and to bless all the work of your hand. You will lend to many nations, but you will not borrow. The LORD will make you the head and not the tail; you will only be above and you will not be beneath, if you listen to the commandments of the LORD your God, which I am commanding you today, to observe and to do them. Also, you shall not turn aside from any of the words which I am commanding you today, to the right hand or to the left, to go after other gods to serve them.

THE LAW OF ABUNDANCE

Although New Agers have tried to claim the law of abundance, it's scriptural. We need not forfeit Bible truths because some unbelievers are working them. Remember, spiritual laws work for "whosoever will." God is no respecter of persons (Acts 10:34). Just as gravity works for all of mankind, God's laws work for all of mankind—for better or worse. We reap what we sow, for example, and the law of abundance works on behalf of those who sow. The difference is that believers have angels of abundant harvest on their team.

The law of abundance basically states that there is enough of everything in the world for everyone in the world. We know assuredly there is no lack in God, the Creator of the universe. The world is His, and all its fullness (Ps. 50:12). The earth is the Lord's and everything in it; the world and all who live in it (Ps. 24:1). He owns the cattle on a thousand hills (Ps. 50:10). The silver is His, and the gold is His (Hag. 2:8). The peaks of the mountains are His, and the sea is His (Ps. 95:4–5). Dominion belongs to Him (1 Chron. 29:11). The heavens are His (Ps. 89:11).

It doesn't sound like there is any lack in the kingdom of God—indeed, there isn't. God can create whatever is needed in the moment. In fact, if He doesn't already have it, He will make it for you. El Shaddai—the God who is more than enough—makes this promise in John 14:13: "I will do whatever you ask in My name, that the Father may be glorified in the Son." That word *will* is one of the strongest words in the human language, so this promise is sure when we ask with right motives.

The late Kenneth Hagin told the story of a scholar visiting a group of young ministers. He was recognized as the leading Hebrew and Greek scholar of his day and was fluent in thirty-two languages.[1] He explained to the group that certain Greek and Hebrew phrases do not correlate to English idioms and used John 14:13 as an example. "The scholar read the verse to us in the original Greek (it was all Greek to me!)," Hagin shared. "Then he said, 'Now I'm going to translate that literally for you.' This is what that verse *literally* says: 'If you will ask anything in My Name, if I don't have it, *I'll make it for you*'!"[2]

We find many verses demonstrating that God does not want His people to lack, and when we obey Him in faith, we will not lack:

- "For the LORD your God has blessed you in all the works of your hands. He knows your wanderings through this great wilderness. These forty years the LORD your God has been with you. You have lacked nothing" (Deut. 2:7).

- "The young lions are in want and suffer hunger, but the ones who seek the LORD will not lack any good thing" (Ps. 34:10).

- "Then He said to them, 'When I sent you without purse or bag or sandals, did you lack anything?' They said, 'Nothing'" (Luke 22:35).

- "There was no one among them who lacked, for all those who were owners of land or houses sold them, and brought the income from what was sold, and placed it at the apostles' feet. And it was distributed to each according to his need" (Acts 4:34–35).

- "If any of you lacks wisdom, let him ask of God, who gives to all men liberally and without criticism, and it will be given to him" (James 1:5).

Scriptures on Abundance Abound

None of this is to say that we will never suffer lack. We reap what we sow for starters, and we know where vision lacks, people perish (Prov. 29:18). We also know Proverbs warns plenty about laziness. Here are just a few of many of those warnings:

- "He becomes poor who deals with a slack hand, but the hand of the diligent makes rich" (Prov. 10:4).

- "The sluggard will not plow because of the cold; therefore he will beg during harvest and have nothing" (Prov. 20:4).

- "In all labor there is profit, but mere talk leads only to poverty" (Prov. 14:23).

Part of sowing is hard work. God has given us the power to create wealth (Deut. 8:18). He's given us the power and ability. God told Abraham, "All the land that you see I will give to you and to your descendants forever" (Gen. 13:15). But Abraham had to take action—he had to look. God told Joshua, "I have given you every place that the sole of your foot shall tread, as I said to Moses" (Josh. 1:3). But Joshua had to do the treading. Again, Deuteronomy 28:8 says God will bless what you set your hand to—but you have to set your hand to it. The fastest way to an abundant harvest is to work hard and sow obediently. This combination can drive miraculous results.

Of course we must not covet abundance. That's the wrong heart. Jesus clearly warned us, "No one can serve two masters. For either he will hate the one and love the other, or else he will hold to the one and despise the other. You cannot serve God and money" (Matt. 6:24). He also said it's more blessed to give than to receive (Acts 20:35). And remember, your faith is the ultimate activator of blessing in your life.

James, the apostle of practical faith, teaches us that when we ask, we must ask in faith with no wavering (James 1:6). But we must be careful not to "ask amiss, that you may spend it on your passions" (James 4:3). Although spiritual laws do not change, we can sow tares in our fields that can allow the enemy in to destroy our harvest. We'll talk more about hindrances to the harvest in later chapters.

Chapter 5

ONLY YOU CAN DECIDE
WHAT YOU SOW

DECISIONS. WE MAKE them every day. Some are good decisions. Some are bad decisions. Some are conscious decisions, and some are subconscious decisions. What will you eat? What will you wear? What will you buy? What will you believe?

The list of everyday choices is endless, and we haven't even included the major life decisions you'll be reaping on for years to come—such as who you'll marry or what job you'll take—or eternal decisions such as salvation, stewarding spiritual gifts, and various other kingdom realities.

By some estimates the average American adult makes 35,000 decisions a day. Decision fatigue—the poor quality of decisions you make over a long season of decision making—is real. In fact, various studies show decision fatigue can trap people in poverty, drive impulse buying, hinder self-control, and even cause you to avoid making tough decisions. You may have heard the term *paralysis by analysis*. This is the rotten fruit of decision fatigue.

Thankfully, when you walk the narrow path that leads

to life, it limits your choices. Casting your cares on the Lord and trusting Him alleviates much of the stress the world feels every day. When we choose to set our minds on things above and not on the things of this earth—when we embrace the reality that this world is not our home, that we're citizens of heaven and seated in heavenly places in Christ Jesus—it does away with much of the fear and anxiety over decision making. At least in theory. We still have to choose to do these things—and we will reap a peaceful harvest from those decisions.

Ultimately only you can decide what you sow. If you sow trouble, you'll reap the same (Job 4:8). If you sow righteousness, you'll reap a reward (Prov. 11:18). If you sow iniquity, you'll reap vanity (Prov. 22:8). If you sow the wind, you'll reap a whirlwind (Hosea 8:7). He who sows sparingly will reap sparingly, and he who sows bountifully will reap bountifully (2 Cor. 9:6). If you sow to the flesh, you'll reap corruption, and if you sow to the Spirit, you'll reap eternal life (Gal. 6:8).

Are you getting the picture? Only you can decide what you will sow. God makes the sun to rise on the good and evil and sends rain to both the righteous and the unrighteous (Matt. 5:45). By God's grace you may receive blessings from the hands of others you did nothing to deserve. You may face a tragic event in your life based on bad seed sown by another, as I did. You may inherit generational curses that must be broken. You may inherit a fortune for which you didn't work. But ultimately your decisions frame most of your life. Whatever happens to you, you still have the ability to decide how you will respond. You can still sow a good seed.

UNDERSTANDING THE POWER OF A DECISION

Although reaping and sowing is a spiritual law, the power of a decision correlates to this spiritual law every day. The most powerful decision you can make is to accept Jesus Christ, the Son of the Living God, as your Lord and Savior. But that opens up a world of eternal possibilities to the one who sows according to the kingdom principles I just shared. Taking up your cross and following Christ is a daily decision. Paul put it best: "I die daily" (1 Cor. 15:31). You must choose every day to sow to the Spirit instead of the flesh.

Today the Lord is calling you to the Valley of Shechem. The Valley of Shechem is where Joshua called together all the tribes of Israel. Once all the elders, chiefs, judges, and officers arrived and presented themselves before God, Joshua delivered a powerful prophetic word to the nation. Joshua prophesied about Abraham, a prophet who once worshipped other gods. He prophesied about the plagues on Egypt. He prophesied about the parting of the Red Sea. He essentially offered a history of Israel right up to its modern day. God was reminding them of the kind intentions of His will.

> Now fear the LORD, and serve Him with sincerity and faithfulness. Put away the gods your fathers served beyond the River and in Egypt. Serve the LORD. If it is displeasing to you to serve the LORD, then choose today whom you will serve, if it should be the gods your fathers served beyond the River or the gods of the Amorites' land where you are now living. Yet as for me and my house, we will serve the LORD.
>
> —JOSHUA 24:14–15

That's a decision! And it was a powerful one. Some of your decisions are more powerful than others—but they all carry weight. The power of death and life are in the tongue (Prov. 18:21). Likewise, decisions can bring death or life to your doorstep.

You can decide to walk in the joy of the Lord, which is your strength (Neh. 8:10). You can decide to pursue a lifestyle of health and wholeness and avoid many of the sicknesses and diseases that plague our generation. You can decide to go to a church that is going to challenge and inspire you to grow instead of one that just feeds you a warm bottle of milk. You can decide to spend quality time with your family instead of pursuing worthless activities. You can decide to fellowship with the Holy Spirit and walk with Him instead of walking in the soul and flesh.

FAITH WITHOUT WORKS IS DEAD

You can decide—and there is power in your decision because you always reap what you sow. Now once you have made a decision, it's important that you stick to it. A decision to lose weight, to sow seed into the kingdom, to pursue a new career path—any decision you make loses power without action. This is also a spiritual principle from James 2:14–26:

> What does it profit, my brothers, if a man says he has faith but has no works? Can faith save him? If a brother or sister is naked and lacking daily food, and one of you says to them, "Depart in peace, be warmed and filled," and yet you give them nothing that the body needs, what does it profit? So faith by itself, if it has no works, is dead.
>
> But a man may say, "You have faith and I have works."
>
> Show me your faith without your works, and I will show you my faith by my works. You believe that there is one God; you do well. The demons also believe and tremble.
>
> But do you want to be shown, O foolish man, that faith without works is dead? Was not Abraham our father justified by works when he offered his son Isaac on the altar? Do you see how faith worked with his works, and by works faith was made perfect? The Scripture was fulfilled

which says, "Abraham believed God, and it was reckoned to him as righteousness," and he was called the friend of God. You see then how by works a man is justified, and not by faith only.

Likewise, was not Rahab the prostitute justified by works when she received the messengers and sent them out another way? As the body without the spirit is dead, so faith without works is dead.

Now if your decision is bearing bad fruit, you may need to make a course adjustment. But remember this: not making a decision is making a decision. Theodore Roosevelt, the twenty-sixth president of the United States, once said: "In any moment of decision, the best thing you can do is the right thing, the next best thing is the wrong thing, and the worst thing you can do is nothing."[1] That's largely true except in the matter of sin. Better not to do the wrong thing! But you understand the principle.

The timing of your decisions is also important. The late *Hour of Power* televangelist Robert H. Schuller offered words of wisdom in this regard, "Never cut a tree down in the wintertime. Never make a negative decision in the low time. Never make your most important decisions when you are in your worst moods. Wait. Be patient. The storm will pass. The spring will come."[2]

Although sometimes you have to make big decisions in trying times, giving up is usually not God's way. Guard your heart and your decisions in times of trial and great emotional stress. There is safety in the counsel of many (Prov. 11:14).

MAKING MONEY DECISIONS

Throughout this book we will speak of sowing and reaping in terms of all matters of life, but finances are part of the abundant harvest. With that, it's important to remember what the Bible teaches about money. Money itself is not a root of all evil—the love of money is where you can go awry (1 Tim. 6:10). David, Solomon, and other servants of God in the Bible were wealthy, and indeed the Bible tells us God has given us the power to create wealth—to establish His covenant (Deut. 18:8). As I said in an earlier chapter—and it bears repeating—our motives matter.

When you make money decisions, make them the same way you would make every other decision—with the counsel of the Word, with the godly counsel of those wiser than you, and as unto the Lord. Cultivate an eternal perspective. Consider your eternal rewards. Reject poverty mind-sets and fear of obeying God in the area of your finances. In the parable of the talents a man gave his servants talents according to their ability. One of those servants did not make a decision but buried the talent in the ground.

> His master answered, "You wicked and slothful servant! You knew that I reap where I have not sown, and gather where I have not winnowed.

Then you ought to have given my money to the bankers, and at my coming I should have received what was my own with interest. So take the talent from him, and give it to him who has ten talents. For to everyone who has will more be given, and he will have an abundance. But from him who has nothing, even what he has will be taken away."

—MATTHEW 25:26–29

If you want abundance, don't bury your talent—or your money. Sow it into kingdom purposes for the glory of God. Here's another truth that bears repeating and expounding upon as the Lord releases the angels of abundant harvest. Jesus made it clear in Matthew 6:24–33:

No one can serve two masters. For either he will hate the one and love the other, or else he will hold to the one and despise the other. You cannot serve God and money.

Therefore, I say to you, take no thought about your life, what you will eat, or what you will drink, nor about your body, what you will put on. Is not life more than food and the body than clothing? Look at the birds of the air, for they do not sow, nor do they reap, nor gather into barns. Yet your heavenly Father feeds them. Are you not much better than they? Who among you by taking thought can add a cubit to his stature?

Why take thought about clothing? Consider the lilies of the field, how they grow: They neither work, nor do they spin. Yet I say to you that even Solomon in all his glory was not dressed like one of these. Therefore, if God so clothes the grass of the field, which today is here and tomorrow is thrown into the oven, will He not much more clothe you, O you of little faith? Therefore, take no thought, saying, "What shall we eat?" or "What shall we drink?" or "What shall we wear?" (For the Gentiles seek after all these things.) For your heavenly Father knows that you have need of all these things. But seek first the kingdom of God and His righteousness, and all these things shall be given to you.

With every decision you make, let Matthew 6:33 be your ultimate guide: seek the kingdom and His righteousness, and you'll tap into the abundant life.

Chapter 6

YOU REAP THE SAME KIND OF SEEDS YOU SOW

IT DOESN'T TAKE an agricultural expert to understand that we reap a specific harvest based on the specific seeds we've sown. If you sow apple seeds, you'll see a harvest of apple trees—not watermelons. If you sow corn seeds, you'll reap ears of corn—not grapes. If you sow judgment, you'll reap judgment—not mercy (Matt. 7:2). If you sow trouble, you'll reap trouble—not peace (Job 4:8).

During the days of Creation God commanded everything to produce after its kind (Gen. 1:11–12, 21, 24–25). What's true in the physical world is true in the spiritual world. A law is a law is a law. We can repent for the bad seeds we've sown, and God will forgive us, but sometimes we still face the consequences of our actions. This is perhaps best illustrated in the life of King David.

David coveted Uriah's wife, Bathsheba (2 Sam. 11:2–3), which violated the tenth commandment. He committed adultery (2 Sam. 11:4), which breached the seventh commandment. He murdered Uriah (2 Sam. 11:15), which broke the sixth commandment. He stole (2 Sam. 11:4), which trampled the eighth commandment. Finally he bore false witness (2 Sam. 11:8, 21), which betrayed the ninth commandment.

The bad news is that although he repented, David would reap trouble in his family line. Solomon wound up serving false gods. One of his sons raped one of his daughters. Absalom launched an insurrection against him and slept with his concubines. The good news is that God still called David a man after His own heart (1 Sam. 13:14). He didn't blot that descriptor from the Bible just because David fell into a whirlwind of sin.

MERCY TRIUMPHS OVER JUDGMENT

We need to be careful to work out our salvation with fear and trembling, knowing that we will reap the same kind of seed as we sow (Gal. 6:7; Phil. 2:12). But we must never forget the mercy of God. The blood of Jesus is sufficient for our sin. When judgment fell on David for taking a census of Israel and Judah, God gave him three choices for the consequences of his sin: seven years of famine, three months running from his enemies as they pursue him, or three days of plague in the land (2 Sam. 24:13).

"David said to Gad, 'I am very distressed. Let us fall by the hand of the LORD, for His mercy is great. May I not fall by the hand of man'" (2 Sam. 24:14). God's mercy is greater than we can realize. That doesn't negate the law of sowing and reaping, but God ultimately chooses the harvest. If we are quick to repent with a sincere heart, it moves Him toward mercy. David understood this, declaring: "For You do not desire sacrifice, or I would give it; You do not delight in burnt offering. The sacrifices of God are a broken spirit; a broken and a contrite heart, O God, You will not despise" (Ps. 51:16–17).

We should not take sin lightly. We should not purposely sow bad seeds in our relationships, health, or any other area of our life. Likewise, we should not withhold the seed when the Lord tells us to sow. If we are continually stiff-necked and rebellious, sowing the wrong seeds and disobeying His prompting to sow the right seeds— such as love, peace, joy, tithes, and offerings—we're tying His hands. The law of sowing and reaping must roll out. This is perhaps best illustrated in Psalm 7:12–16:

> If one does not repent, God will sharpen His sword; He has bent His bow and made it ready. He has prepared for Himself deadly weapons; He makes His arrows flaming shafts. The wicked man writhes in pain of iniquity; he has conceived mischief and brought forth falsehood. He who digs a hole and hollows it will then fall into his own pit. His mischief will return on his own head; his violence will descend on the crown of his own head.

Thankfully mercy triumphs over judgment (James 2:13). The pathway to God's mercy is repentance. David understood this, writing:

Blessed is he whose transgression is forgiven, whose sin is covered. Blessed is the man against whom the Lord does not count iniquity, and in whose spirit there is no deceit. When I kept silent, my bones wasted away through my groaning all day long. For day and night Your hand was heavy on me; my strength was changed into the drought of summer. Selah. I acknowledged my sin to You, and my iniquity I did not conceal. I said, "I will confess my transgressions to the Lord," and You forgave the iniquity of my sin. Selah

—Psalm 32:1–5

Take a moment to ask yourself, what kinds of seeds have I sown? What abundant harvest is about to come into my life? If you've made wrong choices, now is the time to repent and believe in our merciful God.

Chapter 7

YOU REAP IN A FUTURE SEASON

SOMETIMES WE GET what seems to be an immediate harvest from a seed we've sown—for better or worse. I've heard many stories of people sowing their last few dollars, believing God for a financial breakthrough, and getting an unexpected check in the mail three days later.

There are two explanations for this: (1) God is sovereign and can supersede the laws of the harvest, or (2) you're actually reaping a harvest on seeds you sowed in a past season and God decided to bring the harvest in His perfect timing. Either way, I do believe in sowing emergency seeds—and I also believe it is by faith and patience that we inherit the promises of God (Heb. 6:12). Ultimately you can sow and water, but God brings the increase (1 Cor. 3:7).

God gives us insight into the harvest in Genesis 8:22: "While the earth remains, seedtime and harvest, cold and heat, summer and winter, and day and night will not cease." Just like in the natural realm, there is a space of time between the planting and the harvest. Again, although God is sovereign, understanding that we'll reap in a future season is vital lest we grow impatient and lose heart, failing to diligently water our seeds with our prayers and the confession of our heart. Let's look at the Holy Spirit's exhortation at the end of the spiritual law on sowing and reaping in context:

> Be not deceived. God is not mocked. For whatever a man sows, that will he also reap. For the one who sows to his own flesh will from the flesh reap corruption, but the one who sows to the Spirit will from the Spirit reap eternal life. And let us not grow weary in doing good, for in due season we shall reap, if we do not give up. Therefore, as we have opportunity, let us do good to all people, especially to those who are of the household of faith.
>
> —Galatians 6:7–10

When Your Due Season Comes

In the context of the prophecy upon which this book is based, the due season is here. We have reached a tipping point, a *kairos* time. God is releasing His angels of abundant harvest. This will not be the first season of harvest, and it won't be the last season of harvest, but it is important that we recognize the season so we can respond appropriately. And we have to remember that even during times of harvest we're still sowing toward the future.

Again, I believe we are in a *kairos* moment in the body of Christ. I believe this is your time and my time. The Greek word *kairos* means "a fitting season, opportunity, time, occasion."[1] It comes from the Greek word *kara*, "referring to things 'coming to a head'; to take full advantage of."[2] *Kairos* is "the suitable time, the right moment, a favorable moment."[3]

We need to be like the sons of Issachar, having understanding of the times. (See 1 Chronicles 12:32.) We should rightly discern the signs of the times, but we should also press into God's will for this time in our lives. We are living in perhaps the most critical turning point in human history. Christ's coming is sooner than it has ever been, and a tsunami of perversion is rising in this nation and others.

Everything is coming to a head. We need to take full advantage of this suitable, right, and favorable moment. We need to embrace this *kairos* moment and believe that God has called us for such a time as this to do something He uniquely created us to do. We need to prophetically exercise the Isaiah 22:22 key and open what God wants opened and shut what God wants shut.

With the angels of abundant harvest released, we still have to do our part. We need to pray, prepare, and declare. But we must garner a sense of urgency about the moment. For everything there is a season and a time for every purpose under heaven. (See Ecclesiastes 3:1.) In this season God is releasing His angels of abundant harvest.

Chapter 8

YOU REAP EXPONENTIALLY
WHAT YOU SOW

E VERY FARMER UNDERSTANDS the principle that we reap exponentially what we sow—or they would never sow. The reality is that if you sow an apple seed, it yields an apple tree with countless apples and countless more seeds. Although the apple seed is tiny, when it is planted and watered, a tree grows that feeds many. There is a multiplication effect when you sow seed into the ground.

Every day you are sowing seeds from which you will one day reap an exponential harvest. Whether it's kindness, finances, the gospel, or some other seed, you can expect to see this multiplying effect manifest in your life. In this season God is not just adding to—He's multiplying. Whoever has ears to hear, let him hear what Jesus said in the parable of the sower: "Other seeds fell into good ground and produced grain: a hundred, sixty, or thirty times as much" (Matt. 13:8).

One key to the abundant harvest is sowing in obedience. We find this playing out in Genesis 26 in the life of Isaac. In those days there was a famine in the land. Isaac decided to go talk to the Philistine king Abimelek in Gerar. That was a good move, and the Lord confirmed his decision: "'Do not go down to Egypt. Live in the land of which I will tell you. Sojourn in this land, and I will be with you and will bless you; for I will give to you and all your descendants all these lands, and I will fulfill the oath which I swore to Abraham your father. I will make your descendants multiply as the stars of the heavens and will give your descendants all these lands. By your descendants all the nations of the earth will be blessed, because Abraham obeyed Me and kept My charge, My commandments, My statutes, and My laws.' So Isaac lived in Gerar" (Gen. 26:2–6).

Isaac wasn't perfect. Thank God the Lord doesn't demand perfection. While in Gerar he made the same mistake as his father, Abraham. He lied. He told the men in the city that Rebekah was his sister instead of his wife because he was afraid they would kill him to get to her. When Abimelek discovered Isaac's lie, he confronted Isaac and rebuked him, then charged no man to touch Rebekah. Look what happened next.

> Then Isaac sowed in that land and reaped in the same year a hundredfold; the LORD blessed him. The man became rich and continued to prosper until he became very wealthy. For he had possessions of flocks and herds and a great number of servants so that the Philistines envied him. For the Philistines had stopped up all the wells which his father's servants had dug in the days of Abraham his father by filling them with dirt.

Abimelek said to Isaac, "Go away from us, for
you are much more powerful than we are."
—Genesis 26:12–16

Isaac tapped into the hundredfold anointing—and an
accelerated harvest! Indeed, Isaac reaped an abundant
harvest during times of famine, not because he was perfect but because of his overarching obedience to stay in
the land of Gerar. The Lord promises, "If you are willing
and obedient, you shall eat the good of the land" (Isa.
1:19).

There is a place of provision for you. For all the talk
of doom and gloom and economic collapse, we must not
fear what is coming in the days ahead. Ecclesiastes 11:4
warns, "He who observes the wind will not sow, and he
who regards the clouds will not reap." Don't look at the
signs of the times in relation to your financial sowing—
look to the Word of God.

If we want to see the angels of abundant harvest
released in our lives, we must obey the Lord and sow
where He tells us to sow, when He tells us to sow, and
how much He tells us to sow. Don't let fear rob your harvest! Be willing to obey whatever the Lord tells you to do.
Sow obedience and you will reap a good harvest in every
area of your life.

Chapter 9

YOU REAP ACCORDING TO THE PROPORTION OF YOUR FAITH

IT TAKES FAITH to give generously, especially when you don't have much to give. I think of the widow and her mite. Jesus watched as the rich gave gifts out of their abundance while the poor widow gave all that she had. And He esteemed her offering as greater.

Sacrificial giving in faith sets the stage for an abundant harvest. The Word of God with regard to financial prosperity—not the prosperity gospel, mind you, but what the Bible actually says about giving and receiving—should inspire faith in your heart to give.

Although the spiritual law of sowing and reaping is intact, your unbelief can hinder your abundant harvest of blessing just like your repentance can lessen the severity of God's discipline in your life when you sow the wrong seeds. Consider Paul's exhortation to the saints at Corinth:

> But this I say: He who sows sparingly will also reap sparingly, and he who sows bountifully will also reap bountifully. Let every man give according to the purposes in his heart, not

grudgingly or out of necessity, for God loves a cheerful giver. God is able to make all grace abound toward you, so that you, always having enough of everything, may abound to every good work. As it is written:

"He has dispersed abroad, He has given to the poor; His righteousness remains forever."

Now He who supplies seed to the sower and supplies bread for your food will also multiply your seed sown and increase the fruits of your righteousness. So you will be enriched in everything to all bountifulness, which makes us give thanks to God.

For the administration of this service not only supplies the need of the saints, but is abundant also through many thanksgivings to God. Meanwhile, through the performance of this ministry, they glorify God for the profession of your faith in the gospel of Christ and for your liberal sharing with them and with all others. And in their prayer for you, they long for you because of the surpassing grace of God in you. Thanks be to God for His indescribable gift.

—2 CORINTHIANS 9:6–15

WHAT THE BIBLE SAYS ABOUT GIVING

Money is a central theme in the Bible. In fact, Jesus talked more about money than He taught on heaven or hell. Eleven of the thirty-nine parables He shared concern finances. I'm not going to share here an exhaustive list of what the Bible teaches on giving, but here are a few verses in the context of sowing and reaping that are important in light of the Lord releasing the angels of abundant harvest.

- "You must surely give to him, and your heart shall not be grieved when you give to him, because in this thing the LORD your God will bless you in all your works, and in all that you put your hand to do" (Deut. 15:10).

- "There is one who scatters, yet increases; and there is one who withholds more than is right, but it leads to poverty. The generous soul will be made rich, and he who waters will be watered also himself" (Prov. 11:24–25).

- "He covets greedily all the day long, but the righteous gives and does not spare" (Prov. 21:26).

- "Bring all the tithes into the storehouse, that there may be food in My house, and test Me now in this, says the LORD of Hosts, if I will not open for you the windows of heaven and pour out for you a blessing, that there will not be room enough to receive it" (Mal. 3:10).

- "Give, and it will be given to you: Good measure, pressed down, shaken together, and

running over will men give unto you. For
with the measure you use, it will be measured unto you" (Luke 6:38).

- "In all things I have shown you how, working
  like this, you must help the weak, remem-
  bering the words of the Lord Jesus, how
  He said, 'It is more blessed to give than to
  receive'" (Acts 20:35).

- "Now He who supplies seed to the sower and
  supplies bread for your food will also multiply your seed sown and increase the fruits
  of your righteousness" (2 Cor. 9:10).

You have to decide: Is God's Word true, or is He a liar?

GIVE WITH THE RIGHT MOTIVES

The so-called prosperity gospel perverts the Scriptures
for personal gain. In all your giving, give with a right
motive. Although you can expect to reap what you sow,
and it's OK to sow a seed and believe God for increase,
ultimately we need to do everything for the glory of God.

Just as we love God because He first loved us (1 John
4:19), we give as unto the Lord because He gave to us.
Jesus said, "For God so loved the world that He gave His
only begotten Son, that whoever believes in Him should
not perish, but have eternal life" (John 3:16).

God is a giver—and His motives are pure. He gives
us the power to create wealth to establish His covenant

on the earth (Deut. 8:18). He has given us His Son, His name, His blood, His weapons, His righteousness, His love, His faithfulness, and more. He saved us from the kingdom of darkness. He blessed us with every spiritual blessing in Christ (Eph. 1:3).

As Paul said, "God loves a cheerful giver" (2 Cor. 9:7). If God has your whole heart, your finances shouldn't be an issue of contention. Jesus said, "Where your treasure is, there will your heart be also" (Matt. 6:21). Worshipping Him in spirit and truth is more than offering a sacrifice of praise—it's worshipping Him in our giving.

Don't give with a religious mind-set—to be seen of men or just hoping to get a strategic return on an investment. Give in faith for His glory. Give with compassion. Give sacrificially. Give with eternity in mind. Give because you love the Lord.

Chapter 10

YOU REAP GOOD THINGS
WHEN YOU DON'T GIVE UP

I HOP's MISTY EDWARDS sings a song that always stirs my heart on down days. It's called "Turn It All Around." In it she urges us not to give up or give in, declaring we will win if we don't quit.

Whatever you have been sowing toward, now is not the time to give up and give in. Now is the wrong time to throw in the towel in discouragement. Indeed, now is the time to press. Now is the time to pull the weeds of doubt, unbelief, fear, and discouragement out of the soil of your soul and only believe.

See, sometimes the enemy comes behind you and sows tares in your field. Those tares often come in the form of vain imaginations in your mind. The enemy wants to tell you that God won't do for you what He did for someone else. The enemy wants to suggest that you would be better off sowing to your bank account for a rainy day. The enemy whispers all manner of lies that aim to cause you not to till the field. Consider Paul's words to Timothy: "Endure hard times as a good soldier of Jesus Christ" (2 Tim. 2:3). Hard times will come. Those who weed their gardens will see a breakthrough.

If you have to weed through pain and water through tears, persevere. Psalm 126:5 promises, "Those who sow in tears shall reap in joy."

"No soldier on active duty entangles himself with civilian affairs, that he may please the enlisting officer" (2 Tim. 2:4). Don't listen to what the newsman has to say about the economy. Don't listen to what the conspiracy theorists say about the government. Stay focused on what the Lord told you to do. Sow faith seeds, not fear seeds. Deuteronomy 22:9 says, "You must not sow your vineyard with two kinds of seeds, or the fruit of your seed which you have sown and the fruit of your vineyard will be defiled." There is a principle here worth noting. Seeds of fear will defile your vineyard. If you have been in fear, repent.

"Anyone who competes as an athlete is not rewarded without competing legally" (2 Tim. 2:5). Consider the spiritual laws of the kingdom as you race toward your reward—not just the law of sowing and reaping, but all the laws, especially the law of love. Remember, faith works by love (Gal. 5:6).

"The farmer who labors should be first to partake of the crops" (2 Tim. 2:6). When you sow your seed, your work is not done. God is always faithful to do His part, but you still have to do your part. You have to fight the good fight of faith and labor in prayer to get a maximum harvest when you're tempted to give in to the devil's plans for crop failure.

WHEN YOU FEEL LIKE GIVING UP

"Open your ears, God, to my prayer; don't pretend you don't hear me knocking. Come close and whisper your answer. I really need you. I shudder at the mean voice, quail before the evil eye, as they pile on the guilt, stock-pile angry slander. My insides are turned inside out; specters of death have me down. I shake with fear, I shudder from head to foot. 'Who will give me wings,' I ask—'wings like a dove?' Get me out of here on dove wings; I want some peace and quiet. I want a walk in the country, I want a cabin in the woods. I'm desperate for a change from rage and stormy weather."

Those aren't my words. They are the words of King David in Psalm 55:1–8 (THE MESSAGE). But I can certainly relate to those words, and you probably can too.

If you're like me (and David), there are times when you feel like God just isn't listening. Mean voices are rising with guilt and condemnation or angry slander. You feel like you've prayed your guts out. You're battling fear. You just want to fly away, to escape the trial. You want to run off to a cabin in the woods. You need a break from the stormy weather—and you need it now. You've tried everything and nothing changes.

You are on the verge of giving up.

So what do you do when you feel like giving up on your harvest? Do you go on a sleep marathon, hoping to escape the harsh reality? Do you veg out in front of the television with a bag of potato chips and a pint of ice cream (and put on a few pounds), watching anything that will keep your mind off the pain? Do you call your friends to rehearse and rehash the drama, hoping they will have a prophetic word? Do you wallow in self-pity? Do you drown your pillow with tears (Ps. 6:6)? I've done all those things, but none of it helps.

So what should you do when you feel like giving up? You do what David did a few verses later in the same psalm: "I call to God; GOD will help me. At dusk, dawn, and noon I sigh deep sighs—he hears, he rescues. My life is well and whole, secure in the middle of danger even while thousands are lined up against me. God hears it all, and from his judge's bench puts them in their place. But, set in their ways, they won't change; they pay him no mind....Pile your troubles on GOD's shoulders—he'll carry your load, he'll help you out. He'll never let good people topple into ruin....And I trust in you" (Ps. 55:16–19, 22–23, THE MESSAGE).

QUITTING IS NOT AN OPTION

I know all too well what it feels like to want to give up. I know all too well the temptations to revert to the world's comfort in the midst of a trial. I know all too well the emotions that come with a storm raging against your family. But quitting is simply not an option. If we lay our weapons down, the devil won't just forfeit his position and pursue someone else. If we lay our weapons down, we just become an easier target for the enemy. The devil will keep attacking until he has robbed us of our faith to believe in the goodness of God.

When we feel like giving up, we can take our complaints to God. He can certainly handle it. Like David we can take our deep sighs to God dusk, dawn, and noon. But ultimately we have to come to the conclusion that God does hear us (Ps. 116:1), that He is working on the situation (Rom. 8:28), and that His grace is sufficient for us (2 Cor. 12:9). Ultimately we have to conclude God is trustworthy (Ps. 9:10). Ultimately we have to keep on our whole armor of God so we are able to withstand the attacks of the enemy against our mind, and having done all, to stand (Eph. 6:13).

Pile your troubles on God's shoulders. If He carried David's load and helped David out—and He did—then He won't fail you. As trite as it sounds, set your heart to trust in God, and you will not be disappointed (Rom. 10:11). Don't give up. God is releasing the angels of abundant harvest. Now is not the time to quit. Now is the time to let your faith soar.

Chapter 11

BECOMING A FORWARD-THINKING SOWER

I'M A BIG planner. I think strategically. I have life goals, ten-year goals, five-year goals, yearly goals, monthly goals, and daily goals. I am always planning for the future while living in the present—including in the area of sowing and reaping. In my early years as a Christian I did not have a sowing and reaping plan. Honestly, it was only in writing this book that I realized I needed to be more forward thinking in the area of sowing and reaping and started putting into place a strategic, Spirit-inspired sowing plan.

We must be forward thinkers in the area of sowing and reaping. Consider the farmer. Naturally speaking, farmers who see the most yield in their crops are the most prosperous—and they tend to be forward thinkers.

Prosperous farmers plan ahead so they have the right amount of the right seed in the ground during the right season. They understand they need the right amount of water pouring over the fields and the right amount of herbicides on hand. They know they need the right equipment to till the ground and the labor to ultimately harvest the crops—and they need storage for the yield. Modern farmers also have fancy software to help them keep track of the business end of the harvest and, of course, deal with taxes. They have this all planned and plotted out before they ever sow the seed!

What's more, prosperous farmers do not randomly sow based on their current needs alone—they sow into what they will need in the next season. They prepare a long time in advance of the harvest in order to yield the greatest possible harvest. They are strategic thinkers— they are forward-thinking sowers. Successful farmers are patient, knowing that it will take time and hard work to bring in the harvest. But they stick to the plan and do whatever it takes to keep the seed alive from the time they sow until the time they reap.

Consider these wise words from Charles Stanley's *Life Principles Bible*: "Some are deceived because their present seed does not appear to be producing an immediate crop. So they continue down their course, mistakenly believing that there will never be a harvest. But unlike the crops of the field, which get harvested at approximately the same time each year, there is no regular timetable for the harvest of life. Some crops we reap quickly; others take a long time. But do not be deceived—their season will come. And by going the second mile now and giving more than is required, we will reap rich dividends later."[1]

You Can't Turn Back Time

If you haven't been a sower—if you have not given your time, your resources, and yourself—into the kingdom, you can't turn back time. But you can start now. Don't spend time regretting your past choices. If you have disobeyed the Lord in the area of giving—if He's told you to give and you didn't, or if you were ignorant to scriptures leading and guiding you into a lifestyle of giving—then decide in your heart right now to make a change.

Wallowing in guilt, shame, and condemnation, or kicking yourself because you missed the mark is not going to reap a good harvest in your life either. Don't let the devil lock you into a mind-set of regret and rob you of what you could have in the next season. You can't turn back time, but you can begin a forward-thinking journey to sowing and reaping. Be encouraged—you may get a fast return in a season when the Lord is releasing the angels of abundant harvest. Paul's words in Philippians 3:12–15 will help you:

> Not that I have already attained or have already been perfected, but I follow after it so that I may lay hold of that for which I was seized by Christ Jesus. Brothers, I do not count myself to have attained, but this one thing I do, forgetting those things which are behind and reaching forward to those things which are ahead, I press toward the goal to the prize of the high calling of God in Christ Jesus. Therefore let those of us who are mature be thus minded. And if you think differently in any way, God will reveal even this to you.

God doesn't expect us to be perfect. He just expects us to learn from our mistakes. Sometimes we learn obedience through the things we suffer (Heb. 5:8). I know I have, even and especially in the realm of abundance. Let your cry be as the psalmist's cry: "Teach me good discernment and knowledge, for I have believed Your commandments. Before I was afflicted I wandered, but now I keep Your word. You are good and do good; teach me Your statutes" (Ps. 119:66–68).

WHAT'S YOUR GIVING PLAN?

Pray about your sowing and reaping plan—but don't delay. Your next harvest could depend on it. Your plan should always start and ultimately end with prayer, but you can take into account some natural considerations. On the flip side consider how your natural activities are sowing into your future. If you sow to the Spirit, you'll reap life. If you sow to the flesh, you'll reap death. Let these practical steps guide you.

What are you believing God for?
What are your natural and spiritual priorities? You can sow into natural things and reap spiritual things. You can sow into natural things and reap natural things. You can sow into spiritual things and reap natural things. You can sow into spiritual things and reap spiritual things.

What is most important to you in the next season of your life? Is God calling you to launch out into full-time ministry? Pray about sowing into a ministry with a similar vision that is operating with excellence and efficacy. Is God stirring you to start a business? Consider how to bless a non-competing business in your city. What you make happen for someone else, God will make happen for you (Eph. 6:8).

Can you set aside an auto-payment each month with a set amount?

It is easier to plan your giving if you put it in your budget. If you budget to give a set amount to one or more ministries each month, that money will go where you've targeted it. If you don't budget it, that money could wind up going for burgers and fries or some other unnecessary luxury that robs your harvest. Don't get me wrong—there's a time to splurge and celebrate. But forward thinking givers budget their finances.

Consider large one-time gifts.

I've done this a few times in my life and have reaped large results. Remember, you reap what you sow. When I need a massive return, I plant a massive seed.

Now all of this can be taken out of context and seen as a way to manipulate God. You cannot manipulate God. If you ask with wrong motives in your sowing—James calls it asking amiss—you may not get the harvest you are expecting. The spiritual laws of sowing and reaping are still in effect, but God is sovereign and your harvest may come in a way that helps you get your motives right.

Let's look at what the Holy Spirit inspired James to write: "Where do wars and fights among you come from? Do they not come from your lusts that war in your body? You lust and do not have, so you kill. You desire to have and cannot obtain. You fight and war. Yet you do not have, because you do not ask. You ask, and do not receive, because you ask amiss, that you may spend it on your passions" (James 4:1–3).

Sow into good ground.

Whether it's a large or small ministry, sow into good ground. What is good ground? Ultimately it's the ground God tells you to sow into. There may not be much fruit in a small ministry yet, but God sees the end from the beginning. Large ministries can appear to bear fruit, but there may be things behind the scenes you don't see. Remember, man looks at the outward appearance, but the Lord judges the heart (1 Sam. 16:7). Ask the Lord for guidance. He will show you.

Remember what Jesus said as you set out to make your sowing plan: "It is more blessed to give than to receive" (Acts 20:35). This helps you keep your heart right. Although it's not wrong to count on a harvest—we should expect a harvest—and it's not wrong to sow in order to reap, the key is to set our hearts to be generous, cheerful givers as unto the Lord because we love Him, and to give all the more as we increase. When we do, we guard ourselves from the corruption of greedy gain.

Chapter 12

ACTIVATING ANGELIC MINISTRY IN YOUR LIFE

An ABUNDANT HARVEST is at hand," says the Lord. "I am releasing angels of abundant harvest into the nation." God is releasing the angels of abundant harvest, and I believe we need to activate them in our lives. Although we have already activated the law of sowing and reaping by default—it's a spiritual law that works whether we want it to or not—there is an element of faith in standing for your abundant harvest. I believe the enemy has been working against the harvest of many of God's people for years, causing delays, discouragement, and doubt.

Now is the time to get in agreement with the prophetic word. God is releasing angels of abundant harvest into the nation. Will we take Him at His word, agree with Him, align with His purposes, and lift up our shield of faith against the enemies of our harvest? Or will we allow situations and circumstances to cause fear and unbelief to creep in and delay our harvest once again? Whether we believe or not, harvests are coming in this season, but those who activate angelic ministry may find it easier to reap. Those who stand in faith against the wiles of the wicked one to kill, steal, and destroy may sooner see the abundance and overflow.

Although we need to be careful of erroneous teaching about commanding angels, we can activate angelic ministry in our life, according to God's will. Put another way, we can give God something to work with. We can give Him our Spirit-led prayers—we can pray what He tells us to pray so that we are assured an answer. And we can declare His written Word over our lives. We can also wage war with true prophetic words that have come from His heart and know that the angel armies may assist us in bringing His will to pass. Remember, God's Word is His will.

Years ago Billy Graham, my hero in the faith, wrote a tremendous book titled *Angels: God's Secret Agents* that I highly recommend. Reverend Graham tells us, "I do not believe in angels because of the sudden worldwide emphasis on the reality of Satan and demons. I do not believe in angels because I have ever seen one—because I haven't. I believe in angels because the Bible says there are angels; and I believe the Bible to be the true Word of God. I also believe in angels because I have sensed their presence in my life on special occasions."[1]

EMBRACING PSALM 103:20 REALITIES

While writing my book *Waging Prophetic Warfare*, the role of angels in our lives because crystal clear to me. God taught me a lot in that season about Psalm

103:20–21. Let's dig into these verses: "Bless the LORD, you His angels, who are mighty, and do His commands, and obey the voice of His word. Bless the LORD, all you His hosts; you servants who do His pleasure."

Note here that the angels are mighty. The Hebrew word for *mighty* in this verse is *gibbowr*, which also implies strong and brave, according to the *KJV Old Testament Hebrew Lexicon*.[2] Angels are not afraid of demons. They are not afraid of the fight. The angels do—or *asah*—His commandments. The Hebrew word denotes "to do, fashion, accomplish, make, work, deal with, act with effect, produce, prepare, attend to, put in order, and observe."[3]

As you can see, the angels are serious about this business—they are totally dedicated to accomplishing Christ's commandments, or *dabars*. The Hebrew word defines *commandments* as "speech, word, speaking, saying, utterance, and business."[4] The angels are busy about the Father's business. When He utters His will—or when we utter His words as directed by the Holy Spirit— the angels seek to execute the mission for His glory.

The angels are always at attention like good soldiers in an army. Their minds do not wander like ours. They are not slack, and they are not sleeping. The Bible says they obey—or *shama*—His word. They are not those hearers of the word who are not doers and deceive themselves (James 1:22). They don't have to wonder if they really heard from God. They hear clearly, and they obey promptly. *Shama* denotes that they listen, understand, give heed, agree, hear with attention or interest, and yield to.[5] They don't just nod their heads and go float on a cloud somewhere. The voice of the Lord activates them into their assignment.

As employees in the White House serve at the pleasure of the president, angels serve at the pleasure of the King. Angels seek to do His pleasure, or *ratsown*. The Hebrew expounds on this word *pleasure* with definitions including "delight, favor, goodwill, acceptance, and desire."[6] God's will toward us is good. Jeremiah 29:11 reminds us, "For I know the plans that I have for you, says the LORD, plans for peace and not for evil, to give you a future and a hope." The angels are part of God's master plan to bring peace and hope into your life.

Let's look at some other translations of Psalm 103:20–21. Begin even now to meditate on these scriptures to get this truth down in your spirit—and renew your mind from what religion may have taught you about angels.

- "Bless (affectionately, gratefully praise) the Lord, you His angels, you mighty ones who do His commandments, hearkening to the voice of His word. Bless (affectionately, gratefully praise) the Lord, all you His hosts, you His ministers who do His pleasure" (AMPC).

- "Praise the LORD, you angels, you mighty ones who carry out his plans, listening for each of his commands. Yes, praise the LORD,

you armies of angels who serve him and do
his will!" (NLT)

- "Praise the LORD, you his angels, you mighty
  ones who do his bidding, who obey his word.
  Praise the LORD, all his heavenly hosts, you
  his servants who do his will" (NIV).

- "So bless GOD, you angels, ready and able to
  fly at his bidding, quick to hear and do what
  he says. Bless GOD, all you armies of angels,
  alert to respond to whatever he wills" (THE
  MESSAGE).

ACTIVATING ANGELS OF ABUNDANT HARVEST WITH WORDS

So how do you activate your angels? By giving voice to
God's Word. God has given us dominion in the earth.
He's given us His name, His blood, His blessing, His righteousness, His armor—and His Word. Remember, the
angel Gabriel said, "Do not be afraid, Daniel. For from the
first day that you set your heart to understand this and to
humble yourself before your God, your words were heard,
and I have come because of your words" (Dan. 10:12).

The angels respond to our declarations of God's Word
on the earth just like the demonic angels hearken to kill,
steal, and destroy when we agree with and speak out
what the enemy is saying over our lives. The power of
death and life are indeed in the tongue! (Prov. 18:21).

In this often-quoted verse, *death* means "death." It's not a symbolic death. It means death. *Life* means "life," though the Hebrew word *chay* can also be translated "living, alive, revival, and renewal."[7] If you want to see a revival in your life, meditate on and speak the Word! The Word of God is alive. The enemy's words carry death.

The word *power* in Proverbs 18:21 actually translates "hand," according to the *KJV Old Testament Hebrew Lexicon*.[8] Whose hand do you want to see at work in your life? God's hand or the enemy's hand? Your words give the devil something to work with; they give God something to work with; and they give angels something to work with.

In the context of activating the angels of abundant harvest, we would be wise to consider the Spirit-inspired words of James, the apostle of practical faith, in James 3:1–12:

> My brothers, not many of you should become teachers, knowing that we shall receive the greater judgment. We all err in many ways. But if any man does not err in word, he is a perfect man and able also to control the whole body.
>
> See how we put bits in the mouths of horses that they may obey us, and we control their whole bodies. And observe ships. Though they are so great and are driven by fierce winds, yet they are directed with a very small rudder wherever the captain pleases. Even so, the tongue is

a little part of the body and boasts great things. See how great a forest a little fire kindles. The tongue is a fire, a world of evil. The tongue is among the parts of the body, defiling the whole body, and setting the course of nature on fire, and it is set on fire by hell.

All kinds of beasts, and birds, and serpents, and things in the sea are tamed or have been tamed by mankind. But no man can tame the tongue. It is an unruly evil, full of deadly poison.

With it we bless the Lord and Father, and with it we curse men, who are made in the image of God. Out of the same mouth proceed blessing and cursing. My brothers, these things ought not to be so. Does a spring yield at the same opening sweet and bitter water? Can the fig tree, my brothers, bear olives, or a vine, figs? So no spring can yield both salt water and fresh water.

In this season when the Lord is releasing the angels of abundant harvest, we need to be ever mindful of our words. We need to decree and declare His Word and activate the angels rather than decreeing and declaring the enemy's words and activating demonic activity in our life that could hinder our harvest. Decree the word of the Lord. Give the angels an assignment.

Remember Isaiah 55:10–11: "For as the rain comes down, and the snow from heaven, and do not return there but water the earth and make it bring forth and bud that it may give seed to the sower and bread to the eater, so shall My word be that goes forth from My mouth; it shall not return to Me void, but it shall accomplish that which I please, and it shall prosper in the thing for which I sent it."

THE LAW OF BINDING AND LOOSING

We can also use the law of binding and loosing in relation to activating the angels. If you run in spiritual warfare circles, you are probably familiar with this principle Jesus shared in Matthew 18:18: "Truly I say to you, whatever you bind on earth will be bound in heaven, and whatever you loose on earth will be loosed in heaven."

The Greek word for *bind* in this verse is *deo*. According to the *KJV New Testament Greek Lexicon*, it means "to bind, tie, fasten, fasten with chains, to throw into chains."[9] The devil also tries to bind us as he did the woman in Luke 13:11 who had been crippled by a spirit for eighteen years. She was bent over and could not stand up straight. Jesus loosed her from the infirmity, untying the bonds of the wicked one.

Just as we bind devils, we can loose angels. Now this is not the same as commanding angels. It's rather giving angels the liberty to execute their assignment. It is essentially agreeing with the Word of God and the angelic network assignment to carry forth His will. In other words, if it's not God's will for angels to get involved in a thing, we can loose all day long, but it won't make an impact. The Amplified version sheds some light on this by expounding on the Greek: "Truly I tell you, whatever you forbid and declare to be improper and unlawful on earth must be what is already forbidden in heaven, and whatever you permit and declare proper and lawful on earth must be what is already permitted in heaven" (Matt. 18:18, AMPC).

We can say, "I loose the angels of heaven to bring in the abundant harvest." But if God has not already loosed them in heaven, He is not obligated to heed your voice. In this case we have the prophetic word to stand on: "I am releasing the angels of abundant harvest." Therefore, we can loose the angels in agreement with the will of the Lord. But be cautious about loosing angels willy-nilly in areas of your life without the leading of the Holy Spirit.

The Greek word for *loose* in Matthew 18:18 comes from the word *luo*. According to the *KJV New Testament Greek Lexicon*, it means "to loose any person (or thing) tied or fastened" and "to set free."[10] Sometimes we tie our angels' hands with our words or other grievances, including doubt and unbelief. We need to set them free by faith to do the will of the Lord. We need to loose them to war with us in the battle.

A WORD ABOUT WARRING ANGELS

This is a strategic time to look at a few examples of warring angels in Scripture. Remember when Elisha's servant was nervous about the enemy invasion? Elisha had spiritual discernment concerning the unseen army working on his behalf and told his servant: "'Do not be afraid, for there are more with us than with them.' Then Elisha prayed, 'LORD, open his eyes and let him see.' So the LORD opened the eyes of the young man, and he saw that the mountain was full of horses and chariots of fire surrounding Elisha" (2 Kings 6:16–17).

Daniel had angels warring to bring him a prayer answer. We read about this supernatural battle in Daniel 10:11–15:

> He said to me, "O Daniel, a man greatly beloved, understand the words that I speak to you, and stand upright, for I have been sent to you now." And when he had spoken this word to me, I stood trembling.
>
> Then he said to me, "Do not be afraid, Daniel. For from the first day that you set your heart to understand this and to humble yourself before your God, your words were heard, and I have come because of your words. But the prince of the kingdom of Persia withstood me for twenty-one days. So Michael, one of the chief princes, came to help me, for I had been left there with the kings of Persia. Now I have come to make you understand what shall befall your people in the latter days. For the vision is yet for many days."

We see warring angels in combat in other passages of Scripture. Revelation 12:7–9 states, "Then war broke out in heaven. Michael and his angels fought against the dragon, and the dragon and his angels fought, but they did not prevail, nor was there a place for them in heaven any longer. The great dragon was cast out, that ancient serpent called the Devil and Satan, who deceives the whole world. He was cast down to the earth, and his angels were cast down with him."

Second Thessalonians 1:7–10 states, "When the Lord Jesus is revealed from heaven with His mighty angels, in flaming fire taking vengeance on those who do not know God and do not obey the gospel of our Lord Jesus Christ. They shall be punished with eternal destruction, isolated from the presence of the Lord and from the glory of His power, when He comes, in that Day, to be glorified in His saints and to be marveled at by all those who believe, because our testimony among you was believed."

Clearly angel armies are part of God's battle plan. They war on our behalf—and ultimately on His behalf—to bring His will forth in the earth just as it is in heaven.

A Prayer to Release the Angels of Abundant Harvest

Angels hearken to the voice of God's Word (Ps. 103). We can decree God's will, which we'll talk about in the final chapter, but we can also pray to release the angels of abundant harvest. Here is one caution: God can bring the harvest in however He chooses. We must always allow the Spirit's unction to inspire us to release the angels into ministry. That said, we are in a time when the Lord is releasing the angels of abundant harvest. Here is a model prayer to guide you:

> Father, I thank You for Your wisdom in creating the angels and for Your willingness to send them into service—and into battle—on my behalf. Forgive me for any negative confessions or declarations that have unleashed demons over my harvest, in the name of Jesus, and help me speak words unto which Your angels can hearken.
>
> Father, give me a discerning spirit that senses the presence of angels and Your unction to release them into the harvest or any other situation in my life. Open my eyes to the angelic realm so I can cooperate more fully with Your work in the earth, and help me not to neglect the ministry of angels.
>
> I release angels of abundant harvest and prosperity into my life right now in the name of Jesus. I welcome the ministry of the harvesting angels into my life and finances. I thank You for an open heaven over me where angels are ascending and descending and intervening in the affairs of my life for Your glory.

Lord, loose Your warring angels to war against any enemy that is working to steal my harvest. Release them now in the name of Jesus to bind the strongman, to root out thieving demons, and to otherwise thwart the weapons the enemy is forming against my harvest.

Thank You, Father, that You hear my petitions and declarations. Thank You for releasing the angels of abundant harvest. Thank You for the protection Your angels offer me. Thank You for Your great love for me in the name of Jesus.

Chapter 13

HINDERING ANGELIC MINISTRY IN YOUR MIDST

In a season when the Lord is releasing the angels of abundant harvest, we want to be especially careful to understand what hinders angelic activity. We talk a lot—or at least a little—about grieving the Holy Spirit, but we can also grieve angels. Consider the word of the Lord to Moses in Exodus 23:20–23:

> Indeed, I am going to send an angel before you to guard you along the way and to bring you into the place which I have prepared. Be on guard before him and obey his voice. Do not provoke him, for he will not pardon your transgressions, for My name is in him. But if you diligently obey his voice and do all that I say, then I will be an enemy to your enemies and an adversary to your adversaries. For My angel will go before you and bring you to the Amorites, and the Hittites, and the Perizzites, and the Canaanites, the Hivites, and the Jebusites, and I will completely destroy them.

We know the Israelites grieved Moses, grieved the Lord, and grieved the angels. It took them forty years to make a forty-day journey. No, they did not starve, and their clothes and shoes did not wear out, but they didn't exactly live in abundance. And an entire generation failed to make it into the Promised Land, that land flowing with milk and honey. Let's take care not to hinder angelic activity in our midst.

In a season when God is actively dispatching angels to assist you in bringing in a harvest you can hardly contain, it is vital that we understand the role of angels, how to cooperate with their ministry, and how to avoid actions and words that hinder them.

An Evil Report Hinders Angels

Speaking words contrary to God's will out of frustration, anger, or some other emotion can grieve the angels. We know angels hearken unto the voice of God's Word (Ps. 103:20, KJV). Much the same way, demons hearken unto the voice of our words that don't line up with His Word. Put another way, demons use our doubting, unbelieving, and fearful words to wreak havoc on our lives. Our evil reports about our seed or anything else in our lives hinders the angels and releases greater warfare in the spirit over our harvest.

Think about it for a minute. How would you like to be working as hard as you can to bring in a harvest for someone only to discover that they are working against you every step of the way? Let's not make it harder on the angels of abundant harvest than it needs to be. There is already a war in the heavens without our evil report adding to the behind-the-scenes drama.

Practicing Sin Grieves Angels

We all sin and fall short of the glory of God (Rom. 3:23). If we claim to be without sin, we're deceiving ourselves (1 John 1:8). But there is a marked difference between missing the mark and repenting and willfully wallowing in muck and mire.

Four times in the Bible we read about God's "holy angels." The holy angels are coming back with Jesus in His glory (Matt. 25:31; Mark 8:38; Luke 9:26). The holy angels are present during the judgment in the Book of Revelation (Rev. 14:10). Around the throne of God the angels cry night and day, "Holy, holy, holy, is the Lord of Hosts; the whole earth is full of His glory" (Isa. 6:3). Clearly practicing sin is off-putting to angels just as it is off-putting to the Holy Spirit. Here's my sermon on sinning: If you are practicing sin, stop!

Disobedience May Cause Angels to Oppose You

I imagine at least some of God's holy angels watched Satan fall like lightning from heaven (Luke 10:18). I imagine they saw the wages of disobeying the Lord when a third of the angels followed Satan in his insurrection. Our disobedience offends God's obedient angels. Remember when Balaam set out to disobey the Lord for greedy gain? An angel of the Lord went into action: "The angel of the LORD said to him, 'Why have you struck your donkey these three times? I have come out to oppose you, because your way is perverse before Me. And the donkey saw Me and turned from Me these three times. If she had not turned from Me, surely by now I would have slain you and saved her alive'" (Num. 22:32–33).

While an angel is not likely to slay you in an age of grace, surely an angel can oppose you if you are opposing God's will. That is actually God's mercy in action.

Don't Touch God's Glory

One last thought—taking God's glory can cause angels to rise up and oppose you. Consider Herod's fate in Acts 12:20–23:

> Now Herod was very angry with the people of Tyre and Sidon. But they came to him in unity, and having made Blastus, the king's personal servant, their friend, they asked for peace, because their country was fed by the king's country.
>
> On an appointed day, Herod, dressed in royal apparel, sat on his throne and gave a public speech to them. The mob shouted, "It is the voice of a god, and not of a man!" Immediately an angel of the Lord struck him, because he did

not give God the glory. And he was eaten by
worms and died.

Likewise, King Nebuchadnezzar touched God's glory
and ended up in a wilderness place roaming about like
a madman until he repented (Dan. 4). Again, we are
in New Testament times, not Old Testament times, so
we're not likely to be struck dead or lose our minds for
touching God's glory, but it will hinder angelic activity
in our lives at best. God resists the proud, and pride
comes before a fall.

So when your harvest comes in, be sure to give Him
the honor and glory due His name—and be faithful
to sow from your next harvest. And, I might add, be
mindful of the poor (Gal. 2:10). Remember Proverbs 19:17
in your time of blessing: "He who has pity on the poor
lends to the LORD, and He will repay what he has given."

Chapter 14

FLESHLY AGENDAS THAT
ROB YOUR HARVEST

SOME PEOPLE LIKE to remind me there's not a demon behind every doorknob. I believe that is partially true. Sometimes there is more than one demon behind the doorknob! But many times we blame the devil for the works of our own flesh.

In the parable of the sower Jesus exposes both demonic and carnal agendas that can rob your harvest—as well as the right kind of soil to sow in. We get the revelation in Matthew 13:3–9: "Listen! A sower went out to sow. While he sowed, some seeds fell beside the path, and the birds came and devoured them. But other seeds fell on rocky ground where they did not have much soil, and immediately they sprang up because they did not have deep soil. But when the sun rose, they were scorched. And because they did not take root, they withered away. Some seeds fell among thorns, and the thorns grew up and choked them. But other seeds fell into good ground and produced grain: a hundred, sixty, or thirty times as much. Whoever has ears to hear, let him hear."

Jesus explains the parable in verses 19–22: "When anyone hears the word of the kingdom and does not understand it, the evil one comes and snatches away what was sown in his heart. This is the one who received seed beside the path. But he who received the seed on rocky ground is he who hears the word and immediately receives it with joy, yet he has no root in himself, but endures for a while. For when tribulation or persecution arises because of the word, eventually he falls away. He also who received seed among the thorns is he who hears the word, but the cares of this world and the deceitfulness of riches choke the word, and he becomes unfruitful."

So we see a lack of understanding—in this case about giving—opens the door to the enemy to come in and snatch the seed. A lack of understanding about watering the seed could also apply here, as well as ignorance to the fact that the devil is roaming about like a roaring lion seeking to devour (1 Pet. 5:8). We also see that some are tempted to stop pressing in to the harvest when tribulation comes. They stop sowing and watering and believing the harvest is coming. Then there are those who worry, worry, worry, and those who have greedy gain in their hearts. Both those actions choke out the seed.

Although the enemy does come to steal, kill, and destroy, our own flesh and stinking thinking can contaminate our harvest just as fast as—and sometimes faster than—the direct work of our adversary. There are obvious issues, such as failing to plant the right seed at the right time or planting only part of what the Holy Spirit told you to sow. As I say often, we can't do God's part, but God won't do our part. Partial obedience is ultimately still disobedience. Beyond what we discern from the parable of the sower, let's explore some other fleshly agendas that can rob your harvest.

TAKING UNGODLY COUNSEL

Taking ungodly counsel with regard to your seed can lead you to a crop failure. I am reminded of Psalm 1:1–3: "Blessed is the man who walks not in the counsel of the ungodly, nor stands in the path of sinners, nor sits in the seat of scoffers; but his delight is in the law of the LORD, and in His law he meditates day and night. He will be like a tree planted by the rivers of water, that brings forth its fruit in its season; its leaf will not wither, and whatever he does will prosper."

PRACTICING POOR STEWARDSHIP

In Matthew 25:14–30, Jesus shares the parable of the talents, which is quite telling and needs little explanation but is worth reviewing in a season during which the Lord is releasing the angels of abundant harvest:

> Again, the kingdom of heaven is like a man traveling into a far country, who called his own servants and entrusted his goods to them. To one he gave five talents, to another two, and to another one, to every man according to his ability. And immediately he took his journey.

He who had received the five talents went and traded with them and made another five talents. So also, he who had received two gained another two. But he who had received one went and dug in the ground and hid his master's money.

After a long time the master of those servants came and settled accounts with them. He who had received five talents came and brought the other five talents, saying, "Master, you entrusted to me five talents. Look, I have gained five talents more."

His master said to him, "Well done, you good and faithful servant. You have been faithful over a few things. I will make you ruler over many things. Enter the joy of your master."

He who had received two talents also came and said, "Master, you entrusted me with two talents. See, I have gained two more talents besides them."

His master said to him, "Well done, you good and faithful servant. You have been faithful over a few things. I will make you ruler over many things. Enter the joy of your master."

Then he who had received the one talent came and said, "Master, I knew that you are a hard man, reaping where you did not sow, and gathering where you did not winnow. So I was afraid, and went and hid your talent in the ground. Here you have what is yours."

His master answered, "You wicked and

slothful servant! You knew that I reap where I have not sown, and gather where I have not winnowed. Then you ought to have given my money to the bankers, and at my coming I should have received what was my own with interest. So take the talent from him, and give it to him who has ten talents. For to everyone who has will more be given, and he will have an abundance. But from him who has nothing, even what he has will be taken away. And throw the unprofitable servant into outer darkness, where there will be weeping and gnashing of teeth."

No need to expound here. Let's commit to being wise stewards.

A Lesson From the Lazy

I warned about laziness earlier in the book, but let's look at another example King Solomon shared in his wisdom to drive the point home. We find it in Proverbs 24:30–34: "I went by the field of the slothful, and by the vineyard of the man void of understanding; and it was all grown over with thorns, and nettles covered its surface, and the stone wall was broken down. Then I saw, and considered it; I looked on it and received instruction: yet a little sleep, a little slumber, a little folding of the hands to sleep, so your poverty will come like a stalker, and your need as an armed man."

Weeding your field and bringing in the harvest is hard

work. The spiritual law of sowing and reaping remains true, but Proverbs 10:5 says he who sleeps in harvest is a son who brings shame. Let's not be lazy and sleep during this harvest season!

WORLDLY CARNAL LUSTS

John offers a strong exhortation that we would do well to heed in a season when the Lord is releasing the angels of abundant harvest: "Do not love the world or the things in the world. If anyone loves the world, the love of the Father is not in him. For all that is in the world—the lust of the flesh, the lust of the eyes, and the pride of life—is not of the Father, but is of the world. The world and its desires are passing away, but the one who does the will of God lives forever" (1 John 2:15–17).

We have to wage war on carnal lusts, which, as John revealed, includes more than sexual sin. *Vine's Dictionary* defines *lust* as a "strong desire" of any kind.[1] Although the Bible uses *lust* in a positive context three times, the Word of God most often describes it as a root of sin. Lust is associated with pride, greed, and other strong desires that lead us out of God's will.

Hebrews 13:5 warns, "Let your lives be without love of money, and be content with the things you have. For He has said: 'I will never leave you, nor forsake you.'" And Luke 12:15 admonishes, "Take heed and beware of covetousness. For a man's life does not consist in the abundance of his possessions." But Proverbs 11:24 reveals,

"There is one who scatters, yet increases; and there is one who withholds more than is right, but it leads to poverty."

SEEKING THE HUNDREDFOLD RETURN

Jesus concluded the explanation of the parable of the sower with these words: "But he who received seed on the good ground is he who hears the word and understands it, who indeed bears fruit. Some produce a hundred, sixty, or thirty times what was sown" (Matt. 13:23). This suggests a thirtyfold return is the least you can expect if you hear the Word, understand it, and persevere until it bears fruit. I'd be happy if we stopped there. But it's possible to see a sixty- or even hundredfold return on your seed, which can be far greater than one hundred times as much as you sowed. I believe Jesus was speaking about receiving the greatest possible return. The Lord is releasing the angels of abundant harvest to help us bring in the blessings that have been stored up for us.

Chapter 15

DEMONIC AGENDAS THAT STEAL YOUR YIELD

JEZEBEL STOLE NABOTH's inheritance (1 Kings 21). Jacob stole his brother's blessing (Gen. 27). Absalom stole David's kingdom, at least for a moment in time (2 Sam. 15). Satan comes to devour your seed before it can take root (Mark 4:4). The enemy comes to steal, kill, and destroy your blessing, your inheritance, and your yield. The good news is that you have authority over the enemy. He can't steal unless you allow him an entryway into your life—and when you catch the thief, you can demand justice.

With the release of the angels of abundant harvest, it's time to close any open doors and stand against the demonic agendas that steal your yield. It's time to gird yourself up and put an end to the financial attacks against you. It's time to break the generational curses and vicious cycles that plague you. It's time to bind the hand of the thief and possess your success. Now is the time.

Jesus said, "When a strong man, fully armed, guards his own palace, his goods are peacefully kept. But when a stronger man than he attacks and overpowers him, he seizes all the armor in which the man trusted and divides his spoils" (Luke 11:21–22). It's time to stand against the strongman—or strongmen or strongholds—that is standing against your abundant harvest.

BINDING THE SPIRIT OF POVERTY

Poverty does not glorify God. God wants us to be in health and prosper even as our soul prospers (3 John 2), but the enemy wants to curse our finances and bring lack and the stress that follows in our life. Shammah wouldn't stand for it, and neither should you.

Shammah, the son of Agee, a Hararite, was one of David's mighty men. In the Hebrew language the name *Hararite* means "mountaineer or mountain dweller." But it's interesting to note that this name also sounded like "the cursed."[1] Shammah refused to allow the curse of poverty to come upon him: "And the Philistines were gathered into a troop where there was a plot of ground full of lentils, and the people fled from the Philistines. But he took his stand in the midst of the plot, defended it and struck the Philistines; and the LORD brought about a great victory" (2 Sam. 23:11–12, NASB).

Shammah took his stand, and the Lord brought about a great victory. When we submit ourselves to God and resist the devil, we will overcome the spirit of poverty or any other spirit. The best way to overcome the spirit of poverty is to give generously, activating the law of sowing and reaping in your life. Of course, you may also have to break curses.

BREAKING GENERATIONAL CURSES

Some Christians don't believe in generational curses, but that doesn't make them any less real. Exodus 20:5 says, "You shall not bow down to them or serve them; for I, the LORD your God, am a jealous God, visiting the iniquity of the fathers on the children to the third and fourth generation of them who hate Me." The bottom line is that blessings come from obedience to God and curses come from disobedience to God.

Entire books have been written on generational curses, but here are six things you need to know and do to break them: (1) identify the curse; (2) repent for your sin and the sins of your ancestors; (3) forgive your past generations and ask the Lord to forgive them; (4) break the curse; (5) declare the curse is broken and decree the opposite in your life (in this case financial prosperity); and (6) ask the Lord for His blessings.

DEFEATING DEMONIC CYCLES

Demonic cycles—a phrase I use to describe how demons create and manipulate strongholds in our minds to tempt us to walk around the same mountain over and over again—are real. Demonic cycles are more than just bad habits and can be more difficult to break because you may not even recognize there is a mental stronghold involved in your drama. And you can't break the power of something you don't know is there. With demonic cycles, spirits often work to perpetuate acts of self-sabotage of which you are unaware.

Breaking the power of vicious circles is often a matter of making better choices, but when it is a demonic cycle, you need to identify the imaginations and wrong thought patterns that are allowing wicked spirits to wreak havoc on your life. Ultimately you have to take responsibility for your choices. No demon in hell is stronger than a will aligned with the Word of God. God's grace floods the soul that seeks first the kingdom of God and His righteousness.

In order to break demonic cycles rooted in soulish strongholds, you have to make a purposeful and diligent effort to cast down the imaginations that defy the Word of God. As believers we have the privilege of using God's Word to tear down barriers erected against His truth. We have the power to fit every loose thought and emotion and impulse into the structure of a life shaped by Christ. Our tools are ready at hand for clearing the ground of every obstruction and building lives of obedience into maturity (2 Cor. 10:3–6).

Possessing Your Promised Land

In this hour God wants His people to possess their lands—debt free. The Bible says we are not to owe any man anything except to love him (Rom. 13:8). When you are debt free, the God-given power to create wealth has a multiplication effect because you're no longer paying interest to the kingdom of mammon. In other words, instead of you working to pay off loans, your money begins working for you. Increase comes by the work of your hand instead of just getting by on the sweat of your brow.

Yes, there is a war to possess the land. Yes, there are giants in the land. But the milk and honey in the land are magnificent, and they are waiting for you. Don't be intimidated by the giants of poverty, generational curses, or demonic cycles. Don't speak out an evil report in the midst of financial attacks. Have that Caleb spirit instead of a spirit of unbelief and defeat. After spying out the land, Caleb said, "If the Lord delights in us, then He will bring us into this land and give it to us, a land flowing with milk and honey. Only do not rebel against the Lord, neither fear the people of the land, for they are bread for us. Their defense and the shadow [of protection] is removed from over them, but the Lord is with us. Fear them not" (Num. 14:8–9, AMPC).

Remember Psalm 35:27 (NASB): "Let them shout for joy and rejoice, who favor my vindication; and let them say continually, 'The LORD be magnified, who delights in the prosperity of His servant.'" If the enemy has stolen past harvests, now is not the time to moan and groan and mourn. Now is the time to rejoice as the Lord releases the angels of abundant harvest, believing whole-heartedly that when the thief is found he "must restore sevenfold" (Prov. 6:31, NKJV).

Chapter 16

AVOIDING ANGELIC DECEPTIONS

Penning a book on angels—especially one connected to a prophetic word—would not be complete without exploring the reality of rising deceptions in the realm of angelic ministry. Of course, these deceptions are nothing new. The Bible speaks of them. But these errors are intensifying in the modern church as the New Age movement continues to infiltrate the prophetic.

Few in charismatic circles would deny the reality of false apostles and false prophets in this hour. There are also false teachers, false evangelists, false pastors, false revivalists—and even false christs. The rapid escalation of deception is certainly a sign of the times, but again it's nothing new. Paul warned of demonic angels in a letter to the church at Corinth in a single line: "For even Satan disguises himself as an angel of light" (2 Cor. 11:14). Matthew Henry's Commentary explains Satan can "turn himself into any shape, and put on almost any form, and look sometimes like an angel of light, in order to promote his kingdom of darkness."[1]

There is no light or life in Satan or his angels. There is only darkness and deception. But Satan's angels are deceitful workers. If their accusations and lies against your mind don't lead you astray, they may manifest in illegitimate supernatural encounters. We need to discern, test the spirits, stay watchful, and judge a righteous judgment. Every supernatural experience is not necessarily from God.

Being a student of the Word and cultivating intimacy with the Holy Spirit will guard your heart and mind from deception. Yet even those who walk closely with Him and can recite long passages of Scripture can be deceived.

The nature of deception is you don't know you are deceived. And if you don't think you can be deceived, you already are. I believe in angelic manifestations and appearances but take caution to test all things and hold fast to that which is good (1 Thess. 5:21). I implore you to do the same.

PAUL'S STERN WARNINGS OF ANGELIC DECEPTION

Paul didn't end his discussion of angelic deceptions there. He carried it over into Colossians and Galatians. This was clearly an issue that was on the apostle's heart and mind.

Paul wrote, "Do not let anyone cheat you of your reward by delighting in false humility and the worship of angels, dwelling on those things which he has not seen, vainly arrogant due to his unspiritual mind, and not supporting the head, from which the entire body, nourished and knit together by joints and sinews, grows as God gives the increase" (Col. 2:18–19).

Angels don't want your worship, but apparently it is tempting to worship them when they appear—John fell for this twice. Notice the angel's response in both passages:

> I fell at his feet to worship him. But he said to me, "See that you not do that. I am your fellow servant, and of your brothers who hold the testimony of Jesus. Worship God! For the testimony of Jesus is the spirit of prophecy."
>
> —REVELATION 19:10

> I, John, am he who saw and heard these things. When I heard and saw them, I fell down to worship at the feet of the angel who showed me these things. But he said to me, "See that you not do that. For I am your fellow servant, and of your brothers the prophets, and of those who keep the words of this book. Worship God!"
>
> —REVELATION 22:8–9

REJECTING FALSE GOSPELS AND PERVERTED PROPHECIES

Satan's angels share a different gospel. It is a perverted gospel. It is a gospel of deception. In reality it's not a gospel at all; it is a pack of lies that works to lead you away from the headship of Christ and into supernatural idolatry. It is a false prophetic spirit many times that seduces people away from His heart. In Galatians 1:6–10 Paul wrote: "I marvel that you are turning away so soon from Him who called you in the grace of Christ to a different gospel, which is not a gospel. But there are some who trouble you and would pervert the gospel of Christ. Although if we or an angel from heaven preach any other gospel to you than the one we have preached to you, let him be accursed. As we said before, so I say now again: If anyone preaches any other gospel to you than the one you have received, let him be accursed. For am I now seeking the approval of men or of God? Or am I trying to please men? For if I were still trying to please men, I would not be the servant of Christ."

Some misled, misguided, or false prophetic voices try to please men with messages from angels that are not in any way holy, divine, or inspired by the Lord. The topic of angels is popular in many church circles, in the New Age camp, and even in other religions. We must proceed with caution and great discernment in the angelic realm, staying within the plumb line of the Word at all times, judging experiences, and worshipping God and God alone.

Angels are real, and God sends them on varied assignments, but we must take Peter's sage advice: "Be sober and watchful, because your adversary the devil walks around as a roaring lion, seeking whom he may devour" (1 Pet. 5:8). Don't let an angel of light steal your abundant harvest!

Chapter 17

PROPHETIC DECLARATIONS THAT RELEASE ANGELS

T HERE IS POWER in the Word of God. Heaven and earth will pass away, but His Word will never pass away (Matt. 24:35). His Word is life to all those who find it, and healing to the flesh (Prov. 4:22). His Word will add length to your life and give you peace (Prov. 3:1–2). The grass withers and the flowers fade away, but the Word of God will stand forever (Isa. 40:8). His Word is spirit and life (John 6:63). His Word is truth (John 17:17). His Word is pure, like silver tried in a furnace, purified seven times (Ps. 12:6).

I shared those passages in my book *Waging Prophetic Warfare*. There are two passages in particular that are especially powerful in any discussion of declarations, decrees, and proclamations. Let's revisit this teaching from my last book in light of the release of the angels of abundant harvest. The first one is Hebrews 4:11–16:

> Let us labor therefore to enter that rest, lest anyone fall by the same pattern of unbelief. For the word of God is alive, and active, and sharper than any two-edged sword, piercing

> even to the division of soul and spirit, of joints
> and marrow, and able to judge the thoughts and
> intents of the heart. There is no creature that is
> not revealed in His sight, for all things are bare
> and exposed to the eyes of Him to whom we
> must give account.
>
> Since then we have a great High Priest who
> has passed into the heavens, Jesus the Son of
> God, let us hold firmly to our confession. For
> we do not have a High Priest who cannot sym-
> pathize with our weaknesses, but One who was
> in every sense tempted like we are, yet without
> sin. Let us then come with confidence to the
> throne of grace, that we may obtain mercy and
> find grace to help in time of need.

In this passage the writer of Hebrews warns us against
not believing God's Word. He explains that the Word of
God is alive. The word *alive* in this verse is the Greek
word *zao*. According to the *KJV New Testament Greek
Lexicon*, some of its definitions are "to live, breathe, be
among the living (not lifeless, not dead); living water,
having vital power in itself and exerting the same upon
the soul."[1] The Amplified translation says it is God "alive
and full of power [making it active, operative, energizing,
and effective]" (v. 12, AMPC).

Jesus is alive. Jesus is the Word made flesh. Therefore
it only stands to reason that the Word of God is alive.
When you proclaim the Word of God over your life,

the Holy Spirit can breathe on a situation. The writer of Hebrews calls God's Word "powerful." When you declare the Word during spiritual warfare, it has vital power to bring itself to pass. In other words, the power necessary to accomplish God's declared Word is contained in the Word itself. Words are like containers of power and carry the power of death and life (Prov. 18:21).

But that's not all. The Word of God is also sharp. In fact, it is sharper than any two-edged sword. That means your sword of the Spirit, which is the Word of God, can cut through any weapon that is formed against you. That's why God can so confidently declare that those weapons cannot prosper. This truth is part of our spiritual heritage (Isa. 54:17). Finally, God's Word pierces, or penetrates, the darkness. The unfolding of His Word gives light (see Psalm 119:130), and darkness has to flee when that Word is declared in faith. The Father of lights enforces His Word.

Declarations Over Your Abundant Harvest

Against this backdrop, make it a practice to decree and declare these prayers, scriptures, and confessions over your life in this season when the Lord is releasing angels of abundant harvest.

- You delight Yourself in the prosperity of Your servant. I declare I am Your servant and therefore You delight in my prosperity (Ps. 35:27).

- Let my vats overflow (Joel 2:24).

- Lord, I thank You for peace within my walls and prosperity within my palace (Ps. 122:7).

- I thank You, Lord, that Your favor rests upon me (Ps. 5:12).

- Your Word says You want me to prosper and be in good health even as my soul prospers. I decree and declare that my soul prospers as I delight myself in Your Word (3 John 2).

- You, Lord, supply all of my needs according to Your riches in glory by Christ Jesus (Phil. 4:19).

- All nations will call me blessed, and I will be a delightful land (Mal. 3:12).

- I decree and declare that I am made rich through Christ's poverty (2 Cor. 8:9).

- Lord, bring me into a good land without scarceness and lack (Deut. 8:9).

- As I meditate on Your Word day and night and am careful to do all it says, I proclaim I will find good success (Josh. 1:8).

- As I embrace Your Word, I declare I am like a tree planted by the rivers of water. My leaf does not fade, and I bring forth fruit in its season. Everything I put my hand to prospers (Ps. 1:3).

- Lord, release the wealth of the wicked into my hands (Prov. 13:22).

- I declare I have given and it is given unto me, good measure, pressed down, shaken together, and running over. I have an abundance, and I live in the overflow (Luke 6:38).

- Because I give in obedience to the Lord's directives, the floodgates of heaven are opened over me and I am receiving a blessing that I cannot contain (Mal. 3:10).

- I am blessed coming in and blessed going out. I am the head and not the tail. I am above and not beneath (Deut. 28:2–14).

- Lord, lead me into the land flowing with milk and honey (Exod. 3:8).

- Jesus has redeemed me from the curse of lack and poverty and want. I am blessed in Christ (Gal. 3:13).

- Because I seek first the kingdom of God and Your righteousness, everything else I need will be added to me (Matt. 6:33).

- I declare I receive riches and honor, durable riches and righteousness (Prov. 8:18).

- Thank You, Lord, for teaching me to profit and leading me in the way I should go (Isa. 48:17).

- I declare that You are Jehovah-Jireh, my provider (Gen. 22:14).

- I proclaim You have given me the power to create wealth to establish Your covenant on the earth (Deut. 8:18).

- I declare You are El Shaddai, the God of more than enough. Wealth and riches are in my house because I fear You and delight greatly in Your commandments (Ps. 112:1–3).

- The blessing of the Lord upon my life makes me rich (Prov. 10:22).

- I love wisdom, and I inherit substance; therefore my treasuries are filled (Prov. 8:21).

- Lord, let my barns be filled with plenty and my presses burst with new wine (Prov. 3:10).

- I believe the prophets, and I prosper (2 Chron. 20:20).

- I am Your servant, Lord. Prosper me (Neh. 1:11).

- I declare all grace abounds toward me, that I will have sufficiency in all things and abound to every good work (2 Cor. 9:8).

- The God of heaven prospers me (Neh. 2:20).

- The Lord my God will make my way prosperous (Isa. 48:15).

- Lord, give me land for my inheritance (Ps. 37:29).

- I thank You, Lord, that You reward me because I diligently seek You (Heb. 11:6).

- Lord, anoint my head with oil, and let my cup run over (Ps. 23:5).

- Lord, bring me into a wealthy place (Ps. 66:12).

- Let Your showers of blessing come upon my life (Ezek. 34:26).

- Let me lay up gold as dust (Job 22:24).

- Let me have plenty of silver (Job 28:1).

- Command Your blessing upon my storehouse (Deut. 28:8).

- Let my barns be full and overflowing. Let my sheep bring forth thousands and ten thousands. Let my oxen be strong to labor (Ps. 144:13–14).

- Lord, release riches and honor in abundance as I seek You (2 Chron. 18:1).

- I declare the plowman overtakes the reaper in my life, and the treader of grapes the sower of the seed, and I live in continual harvest (Amos 9:13).

I break and bind every enemy assignment against my finances in the name of Jesus. I break any and all curses of sabotage, poverty, lack, debt, and failure in the name of Jesus. I bind the hand of the thief over my life in the name of Jesus. I rebuke and drive out spirits of the cankerworm, palmerworm, caterpillar, and locust that would eat up my blessings in the name of Jesus. Let every hole in my bag be closed in the name of Jesus. Lord, rebuke the devourer for my sake.

NOTES

Chapter 3
What Are You Sowing?

1.　Thayer and Smith, *The KJV New Testament Greek Lexicon*, s.v. "*harpazo*," accessed November 27, 2016, http://www.biblestudytools.com/lexicons/greek/kjv/harpazo.html.

Chapter 4
Demystifying the Law of Abundance

1.　Kenneth E. Hagin, "Five Things God Wants to Do for You," Kenneth Hagin Ministries, accessed November 27, 2016, https://rhema.org/index.php?option=com_content &view=article&id=258:five-things-god-wants-to-do-for-you &catid=50&Itemid=146.

2.　Ibid.

Chapter 5
Only You Can Decide What You Sow

1.　Brainy Quote, "Theodore Roosevelt Quotes," accessed November 27, 2016, https://www.brainyquote.com /quotes/quotes/t/theodorero403358.html.

2.　Sydney Trent, "Ten Quotations from the Late Rev. Robert H. Schuller That Could Inspire Anyone," *Washington Post*, April 2, 2015, accessed November 27, 2016, https://www.washingtonpost.com/news/inspired-life/wp /2015/04/02/10-quotations-from-the-late-rev-robert-h -schuller-that-could-inspire-anyone/.

CHAPTER 7
YOU REAP IN A FUTURE SEASON

1.   James Strong, *Strong's Exhaustive Concordance*, s.v. "*kairos*," accessed November 28, 2016, http://biblehub.com/greek/2540.htm.

2.   HELPS Word-studies, s.v. "*kairos*," copyright © 1987, 2011 by Helps Ministries, Inc., accessed November 28, 2016, http://biblehub.com/greek/2540.htm.

3.   Ibid.

CHAPTER 11
BECOMING A FORWARD-THINKING SOWER

1.   Charles F. Stanley, "Life Principle 6: The Principle of Sowing and Reaping," InTouch, July 6, 2014, accessed November 27, 2016, https://www.intouch.org/read/life-principle-6-the-principle-of-sowing-and-reaping.

CHAPTER 12
ACTIVATING ANGELIC MINISTRY IN YOUR LIFE

1.   Billy Graham, *Angels: God's Secret Agents* (Nashville: Thomas Nelson, 1995), 20.

2.   Brown, Driver, Briggs, and Gesenius, *The KJV Old Testament Hebrew Lexicon*, s.v. "*gibbowr*," accessed November 27, 2016, http://www.biblestudytools.com/lexicons/hebrew/kjv/gibbowr.html.

3.   Ibid., s.v. "*asah*," accessed November 27, 2016, http://www.biblestudytools.com/lexicons/hebrew/kjv/asah.html.

4.   Brown, Driver, Briggs, and Gesenius, *The NAS Old Testament Hebrew Lexicon*, s.v. "*dabar*," accessed November 27, 2016, http://www.biblestudytools.com/lexicons/hebrew/nas/dabar-2.html.

5.   Brown, Driver, Briggs, and Gesenius, *The KJV Old Testament Hebrew Lexicon*, s.v. "*shama*," accessed November

27, 2016, http://www.biblestudytools.com/lexicons/hebrew /kjv/shama.html.

6.   Ibid., s.v. *"ratsown,"* accessed November 27, 2016, http://www.biblestudytools.com/lexicons/hebrew/kjv /ratsown.html.

7.   Brown, Driver, Briggs, and Gesenius, *The NAS Old Testament Hebrew Lexicon,* s.v. *"chay,"* accessed November 28, 2016, http://www.biblestudytools.com/lexicons/hebrew /nas/chay.html.

8.   Brown, Driver, Biggs, and Gesenius, *The KJV Old Testament Hebrew Lexicon,* s.v. *"yad,"* accessed November 28, 2016, http://www.biblestudytools.com/lexicons/hebrew /kjv/yad-aramaic.html.

9.   Thayer and Smith, *The KJV New Testament Greek Lexicon,* s.v. *"deo,"* accessed November 27, 2016, http://www .biblestudytools.com/lexicons/greek/kjv/deo.html.

10.   Ibid., s.v. *"luo,"* accessed November 28, 2016, http:// www.biblestudytools.com/lexicons/greek/kjv/luo.html.

CHAPTER 14
FLESHLY AGENDAS THAT ROB YOUR HARVEST

1.   W. E. Vine, Merrill F. Unger, and William White Jr., *Vine's Complete Expository Dictionary of Old and New Testament Words,* s.v. *"epithumia,"* 1940, accessed November 28, 2016, http://www.ultimatebiblereferencelibrary.com/Vines _Expositary_Dictionary.pdf.

CHAPTER 15
DEMONIC AGENDAS THAT STEAL YOUR YIELD

1.   "Hararite Meaning," Abarim Publications, accessed December 2, 2016, http://www.abarim-publications.com /Meaning/Hararite.html#.WEGlRfkrIdU.

CHAPTER 16
AVOIDING ANGELIC DECEPTIONS

1.   *Matthew Henry Commentary on the Whole Bible (Complete)*, s.v. "2 Corinthians 11," accessed November 28, 2016, http://www.biblestudytools.com/commentaries/matthew-henry-complete/2-corinthians/11.html.

CHAPTER 17
PROPHETIC DECLARATIONS THAT RELEASE ANGELS

1.   Thayer and Smith, *The KJV New Testament Greek Lexicon*, s.v. "*zao*," accessed November 28, 2016, http://www.biblestudytools.com/lexicons/greek/kjv/zao.html.

CONNECT WITH US!

CHARISMA HOUSE

(Spiritual Growth)

f Facebook.com/CharismaHouse

🐦 @CharismaHouse

📷 Instagram.com/CharismaHouseBooks

(Health)

📌 Pinterest.com/CharismaHouse

REALMS

(Fiction)

f Facebook.com/RealmsFiction